Jewish Mysticism

The Ultimate Guide to Understanding Kabbalah, Merkabah Mysticism, and Ashkenazi Hasidism

Your Free Gift (only available for a limited time)

Thanks for getting this book! If you want to learn more about various spirituality topics, then join Mari Silva's community and get a free guided meditation MP3 for awakening your third eye. This guided meditation mp3 is designed to open and strengthen ones third eye so you can experience a higher state of consciousness. Simply visit the link below the image to get started.

https://spiritualityspot.com/meditation

Contents

Introduction

Jewish Mysticism is an enduring presence in Judaism with its roots in the Hebrew Scriptures and the revelations shared in its books, emanating from the Faith's patriarchs, Abraham, Isaac and Jacob, and the Prophets.

A strong clue as to the shadowy origins of this tradition, lost largely to time, is the Nation of Israel at Sinai. The Jewish people's solidarity and the direct experience of God in this narrative speaks to the esoteric conjoining of the Divine with The People chosen to bear the Word of the one God into the world, in the form of monotheism.

This is the pivotal jumping off point for Jewish Mysticism. In the Rabbinic Tradition, Judaism is understood as a relationship between God and humanity. This exoteric conceptualization of the Divine as something that exists outside humans, directing the action and hearing the faithful's supplications, is challenged by Jewish Mysticism.

In the mystical model, the Divine is "shown forth" in humanity itself. This anthropomorphic panentheism (the idea that all things are in God) is the basis for Jewish Mysticism beliefs and practices, uniting its various expressions and schools of thought.

In this book, we'll be sharing a close examination of Jewish mystical traditions, encompassing Kabbalah, Merkabah mysticism, and Ashkenazi Hassidism. In these pages, I hope I can provide a deeper look into these vibrant and living traditions and their haunting beauty.

The world of Jewish Mysticism is rich, complex, and filled with the wonder of contemplating that which is not beyond us, but which is part of who we are, as people. Let's explore a different way of encountering the mystery of the Divine, giving us a fresh perspective on Chassidism and its many incarnations.

Chapter One: Jewish Mysticism – The Court of the Most High

"The world is full of wonders and miracles, but man takes his little hand and covers his eyes and sees nothing."

Ba'al Shem Tov

When we hear the word "mystic," we may see an elderly man, thin from separating his physical appetites from those of his spirit. His beard reaches to his knees. His hair is long, and he wears a loincloth as he contemplates the vastness of the Divine from the safety of his cave.

Mysticism is an intensely intimate way of approaching God and the knowledge of God, which exists in every Faith tradition in the world. From the Sufis of Islam to the Beguines of Christianity to the Hassidim of Judaism, mysticism is the embrace of the Divine Breath, breathed into humanity at Creation. Formed of the earth and animated with the spirit of our Source, mysticism finds in the Creation narrative of Genesis 1 the truth about humanity's place – that we are genuinely infused with the Divine.

In that status is no arrogance. Rather there is complete humility and in this humility is the true work of mysticism – to spend this human life contacting the Divine source, ever seeking union with it.

Two Distinct Schools with Three Streams

Jewish Mysticism, has two distinct schools. In the one, the intellect is centered. This school of Jewish Mysticism seeks to "work on God's behalf" through understanding. The primacy of the Torah mirrors Rabbinic Traditions, and the foundation of the Ten Commandments as the basis for all that happens in our daily lives. This is called "moderate" mysticism.

In the second school of belief and practice, the intellect is put to one side, as the spirit takes over. "Intensive" Jewish Mysticism seeks a direct experience of the Divine through applying non-traditional practices like meditation and chanting.

While it's difficult to pinpoint the Jewish mystical tradition's precise origins, a close reading of the Hebrew scriptures readily reveals the "bones" of Jewish Mysticism. Visions and direct experiences of the Divine are baked right into this literature. Prominent in these texts is the origin of Merkavah mysticism, as seen in Ezekiel, chapters 1 and 2, and in Isaiah 6. But the tendency may also be read in the narratives of Jacob's Ladder (Genesis 28) and Jacob wrestling with an Angel (Genesis 32:22-32; Hosea 12:4).

The Hebrew word "Merkavah" means "chariot." The vision of the chariot in Ezekiel and that of the throne of the Divine in Isaiah prompted the earliest known expression of Jewish Mysticism, which sought to penetrate the mysteries of these narratives. Known as Merkavah Mysticism, this tradition is later expanded upon in what's called "Heikhalot" (palaces) literature. While Rabbinic Judaism concedes that the Divine Throne may be approached by studying the Torah, midrash, and Talmud, Merkavah mysticism sought a more spiritual, less intellectually defined approach, emerging in the early centuries of the Common Era.

These two schools branch into three streams, regarding their expression via the Kabbalah (the movement's central text).

- Speculative Kabbalah – describing and understanding the world of the Divine

- Ecstatic Kabbalah – seeking union with God

- Magical Kabbalah – invoking God's presence to perfect the soul of the believer.

The Literature

Key literature of Jewish Mysticism will be discussed in this book at more length. But for this chapter, the following is a brief overview.

The Heikhalot literature comes down to us from the earliest layer of what has been recognized as Jewish Mysticism. While some scholars say the movement can be in the Tannaitic period (70-200 CE), others claim it for the Talmudic period (200-500 CE), in Palestine. This collection of literature has been transmitted to us from Babylon during the Exile.

These early Jewish mystics stood outside most Jewish traditions of the day, believing they could ascend to the Throne of the Divine by employing hymns, prayers, and esoteric practices like the invocation of the names of God, creating a state of ecstasy as they did so.

Deeply oriented toward magic in its earliest expressions, intense Jewish Mysticism eventually changed and grew in different directions. These expressions are contained in early Kabbalistic literature, like Sar Torah. The magical elements were purged from later Heikhalot (3 Enoch, for example).

Merkavah Mysticism was also concerned with seeking the origin of the universe. In this pursuit, it drew heavily on Greek philosophy, particularly Neo-Platonism. This syncretic philosophical incursion led to the emergence of the Kabbalah in the Middle Ages.

Gershom Scholem, Hebrew University of Jerusalem's first professional of Jewish Mysticism, was also an acknowledged authority in the field of Kabbalah, even though he was not himself a Hassidic or even an Orthodox Jew. He theorized that the origins of Jewish Mysticism could be traced to the Second Temple period (516 BCE – 70 CE). His research suggested that mystical traditions could be seen between the lines of rabbinical texts which warned against them.

Alternatively, David J. Halperin, Ph.D., has challenged some of Scholem's assertions, and one challenge is of interest about the origins of Jewish Mysticism. He locates these origins in Babylonian sources, specifically about their more magical aspects. For example, the idea of physically traveling to the Divine Throne as Ezekiel and Isaiah do in the Torah is detailed in texts from this region.

Halperin then traces the influence of these texts to the Jewish Holiday, Shavuot, and the exegetical (critical interpretation, especially drawing on companion texts in other Holy literature) traditions associated with its religious celebration in synagogues. Figuring prominently is, of course, the Ezekiel Merkavah narrative, and the focus of Shavuot – the delivery of the Ten Commandments to Moses in Sinai as described in the Book of Exodus. Psalm 68 is also key to this historical interpretation.

The earliest book in the writings of the Kabbalah is the Sefer Yetzirah (The Book of Formation). While scholars have a variety of interpretations, they believe that the earliest elements of this book date to the 2nd Century CE.

Concerned with a speculative examination of how the world came into existence due to the agency of the Divine, the author of the Sefer Yetzirah is said to be the Patriarch, Abraham. This indicates its popular importance and the esteem in which it was held for centuries. Deeply influential in these times, it's understood to be a foundational text in the development of Judaism, rivaling Talmud's influence.

Today, while studied almost as intensively as the Bible itself, Sefer Yetzirah is regarded as a purely esoteric text, native to its mystical context and of little value outside that. Scribal glosses and other alterations to the text make it both difficult to date with accuracy and difficult to understand.

The Zohar (The Book of Radiance) is a companion to Torah, interpreting it in mystical terms. Like Sefer Yetzirah, it stands as part of the canon of Kabbalah. Also, in common with Sefer Yetzirah, the Zohar is attributed to authorship by a biblical figure, namely that of Moses, with the content revealed to him at Sinai. It was then transmitted orally until the 2nd Century CE when it was committed to writing by Rabbi Shimon bar Yohai. These attributions, though, are more spiritual than scholarly.

Scholars believe the Zohar was written in Spain, principally by Moses de Leon, in collaboration with other authors, during the 13th Century. Interestingly, Aramaic was the language selected by de Leon to lend the appearance of belonging to a much earlier time, as this language wasn't in popular use in de Leon's context.

In the Zohar, the sefirot (revealing the traits of the Divine) appears by way of explaining Divine interaction with the world. Other themes include Divine nature and Creation and how evil and sin operate within it. But the Zohar's mystical treatment of Torah is intended to be revelatory of a deeper understanding of the Exile, the First Temple, and the role of the priest there. Prayer, rituals, and liturgy are also discussed in its pages.

Finally – for our overview – is Sefer ha-Bahir (The Book of Brilliance), said to be the foundational text of Kabbalah. Believed to have been written at the beginning of the 13th Century by numerous authors, Sefer ha-Bahir is considered the text from which derived later Kabbalistic traditions. Its name comes from the book's first narrative, which is an interpretation of Job 37:21, referring to *ohr ha bahir* or "bright light" by Nehunya ben ha Kanah, a figure of the Tannaitic period. Again, the text's authors connect it with earlier times, pivotal to developing Judaism.

Edited, redacted, and glossed, Sefir ha-Bahir is not a book. It's a collection of parables that connect to the sefirot in a very unstructured way. These ideas would be developed as the canon of Kabbalah began to be formed.

The Second Temple (516 BCE – 70 CE)

Mystical traditions are not "tame." That's probably one of the most important aspects of mysticism, in general. Moving parallel to traditional structures, they express humanity's relationship to the Divine in a de-institutionalized, highly personal manner.

This may explain that while Jewish Mysticism can readily be detected in numerous examples from the Torah, there is no accompanying body of evidence it was ever practiced or studied in the times concerned.

Rather, over many centuries and through the focused meditations of rabbis, scholars, and other Jews of intense faith, mysticism within the Jewish tradition came to be recognized as a valid and enduring expression of the Faith.

The destruction of the Second Temple in 70 CE by the Romans echoed, in the minds of Jewish believers, the destruction of the First by the Babylonians in 586 BCE. It's not hard to understand how this event might give rise to an elevated communal spirituality, as the Jewish People were exiled to Babylon in its wake. Jewish eschatology posits the establishment of a Third Temple as the jumping-off point for the appearance of the Messiah.

And so, the Temple's destruction, having been lovingly embellished by Herod the Great, signaled an existential and spiritual crisis for the Jews of the day. Having reclaimed their Faith's physical expression and losing it a second time to a different colonialist force,

Jewish Mysticism arose, creating an internal Temple for the Jewish soul.

Merkavah Mysticism, pursuing a Divine vision of God's own chariot, was born in the crucible of this cataclysmic event. It would become the first recognizable appearance of Jewish Mysticism in the First Century of the Common Era.

Chapter Two: Beholding the Mystery

"Ezekiel saw a vision, and he recounted the varieties of Merkavah."

Ben Sira 49:8

The Prophet Ezekiel is key to understanding the roots of Merkavah Mysticism, not only due to his vision but due to his status as an exiled priest in Babylon. The visions described in Ezekiel 1 - 2 were experienced during the First Temple's destruction, so the vision refers to Ezekiel exercising his priestly agency to approach the Divine by spirit. No longer able to exercise that agency in an accustomed manner, he offers an alternative.

Ezekiel is describing a spiritual transformation, in which the First Temple becomes the Merkavah itself, elevated to the Divine realm and approachable by those of intense spiritual union with God.

It's easy enough to see what motivated the earliest layer of Jewish Mysticism as Jews stood in the ruins of the First Temple and, later, in those of the Second. The desire for a utopian, incorruptible, and indestructible Temple could be realized only when that Temple was spiritualized. And so, early Jewish Mysticism was created to fill a need in the souls of the people through its priestly class.

Heikhalot – The Palaces

Rachel Elior is a Jewish philosophy professor at the Hebrew University of Jerusalem and an expert on the early history of Jewish Mysticism. She has identified the Heikhalot literature as descending from antecedents passed down from the Book of Ezekiel, specifically in Ezekiel 1:1 - 28, 3: 12 - 14, 8: 2 - 4, and 10: 1 - 22.

Ezekiel's visions are stupefying. In the first chapter, he describes himself "sitting there among them (the exiles in Tel-abib, now Tel Aviv), stunned, for seven days" (Ezekiel 3: 15b). These visions are of cherubim with human features, bearing the Merkavah and revealing God's glory to the Prophet in Israel, most notably in visions of the First Temple.

These Biblical texts were to form an emerging canon of mystical literature, some of which were discovered during the excavations at Qumran. Among them were the Songs of Sabbath Sacrifice, The Book of Jubilees, 1 and 2 Enoch, and numerous other writings created between the Second Century BCE and the destruction of the Second Temple in 70 BC.

From this collection of writing grew the Merkavah and Heikhalot tradition, none of which was codified (written down and compiled) until after 70 BC. Professor Elior has determined this body of literature was primarily written by members of the priestly class. These members had been prevented from serving in the Temple for anything from political to religious reasons. Referring to themselves by various names like "guardians of the Covenant" or "the congregation of Holiness." These disenfranchised priestly scribes came to be referred to in Heikhalot literature as "descenders of the Merkavah" or "viewers of the Merkavah." These titles refer to establishing the Holiness of the Divine anew as a replacement Temple and these priestly scribes as those who had witnessed the glory of the precincts of God.

This is where things become very interesting. Elior has described these priests, shut out of Temple service, as a movement of opposition against the Temple's hierarchical clerical culture. A breakaway group, they were well-organized, establishing their own Sabbath laws and religious festivals. But with the Temple destroyed, they abandoned their secessionist impulses, turning their attention to mystical interpretations of Temple practice and of the Temple itself. Following that transition, they began the Heikhalot scribal tradition, perpetuating the work of their mystical, priestly movement.

Exiled Jews and their priests sought a means of absorbing the unwelcome ravaging of God's earthly home in Jerusalem by replacing it with one carried not only in their hearts and souls but also in the body of literature created to reflect the new reality. Without a Temple on the mount, only a Temple in the heart was guaranteed to be impervious to all calamity, save physical, human death.

Controversy

The problem with disenfranchised Temple priests is that they're rather determined and have ideas about how to worship, which are generally at odds with their traditionalist, institutionalized counterparts.

And the Merkavah Mystics of the First Century BCE were no different in this respect. With a concept of worship untethered from prevailing demands for specifically set aside time, place, and ritual formulation, they posited that the heavenly Temple was mandated by scripture, as in Ezekiel. They also diverged with tradition from the standpoint of the liturgical (defining the seasons of religious worship) calendar, characterizing it as violating the Covenant between God and his chosen people.

They believed that any calendar associated with religious ritual should be governed by mathematical principles, starting with the number "7" and multiples thereof, guiding the establishment of a liturgical calendar not based on human observation but the eternal truths embodied by numbers. Instead of the lunar calendar used at that time, the breakaway priests recommended a solar calendar, with all religious festivals relating to others in multiples of seven.

The details of the Heikhalot calendar can be read in the Qumran literature, especially in the Book of Jubilees, and 1 and 2 Enoch, among several other examples. According to Divine Law, drawn from the significance of the number seven as laid out in the Genesis Creation narrative, the priests argued that the angels had shared the number seven's divine origin with humanity.

The object of this divergent organization of ritual time was to consecrate Divine time on earth, following a cosmological scheme transmitted by angelic emissaries. They believed this system displayed the most fealty to the organization of the Divine precincts and their rhythms, unsullied by human agency.

Because of the Second Temple's cleaving to a lunar calendar, the early Jewish Mystics believed that the Temple had been defiled. Again, this is a common theme in the Qumran literature, accompanied by the theme that the Temple priesthood was, itself, iniquitous for having perpetuated it.

And this is where we come to the Heikhalot - the palaces - of this disenfranchised priesthood. They believed in an altogether different style of worship - one simultaneously celebrated by both humans and angels. Their identification with the Heavenly Hosts led them to believe that the performance of ritual with angelic participation was the truest form of Judaism and that which most closely honored and mirrored the actions of the Divine.

Seven is the number of Heikhalot - palaces - through which the faithful could ascend to and descend from the throne-chariot of the Divine. This follows the ordering of Creation in the seven days described in the Book of Genesis.

Numerous texts from Qumran feature hymns which depict the angels joined with humanity in worship. At the root of this is the ontological priesthood, by which priests are born, not made. By pointing to instances of angelic-human worship, the disenfranchised priests sought to establish the origins of the priesthood as angelic and, thus, Divine.

And so, the priests who had been barred from Temple service identified themselves with the First Temple priesthood, claiming this earlier version was closer to their own, being based – according to the breakaway priests – on the solar calendar. They proposed that theirs should replace the prevailing model.

This was a three-pronged proposition, encompassing the First (Solomon's) Temple, the cherubim, with their throne-chariot and Ezekiel's Merkavah as the first prong. The second prong was a prototype for their Temple of the spirit and the solar calendar as a reflection of Divine timekeeping. The third was the priesthood in unity with the angels in service of the cherubim. This was their model for worship.

While it's clear that the disenfranchised priests of the Second Temple had an agenda, they also provided a gift to the future of Judaism in their literature and their challenge to the Temple and its clerical hierarchy. While intent on providing an alternative structure to a system they deemed antithetical to the worship of God, they undertook this mission for all the right reasons. While some might see their efforts as self-aggrandizing, there's little question that locating a spiritual home for the Jewish people in their hearts, rather than within the confines of a building, was a concept well ahead of its time. Looking past all the ritualistic prescriptions, this early Jewish Mysticism has endured in various forms over the 2,000 years which have passed since its emergence.

Ma'aseh Merkavah – The Work of the Chariot

Formulated during the Geonic period (589 CE - 1038 CE), the Ma'aseh Merkavah stands as the most descriptive text of Merkavah Mysticism. Part of the Heikhalot literature, this text is rooted in the mystical, esoteric names of God. These are employed as a means of ascending through the seven Heikhalot or palaces, appearing in hymns and elsewhere throughout.

The book's purpose is that of a guidebook of ascension, including instructions as to rituals employed and methods for the invocation of angels.

The work begins as a conversation between two Rabbis, Ishmael, and Akiva, discussing the aspect of the Divine precincts and the spiritual world's mysteries. As the text continues, specific instruction is given as to how to ascend, including specific Divine names to be invoked as "seals." These instructions include fervent prayer and a casting off the world, embodied in instructions to look at the ground and too fast for 40 days. The student is also instructed to undergo 24 immersions in the mikveh (ritual bath).

There is also a prayer of protection from the Angel of Presence, an angelic emissary called upon as part of the ascent to the heavenly precincts. The power of this angel was considered potentially fatal.

Because of Ezekiel's visionary experiences, the Ma'aseh Merkavah is designed to both interpret and replicate those experiences. By standing in the place of the Prophet, the practitioner realizes the ascent as an eternal reality, available to the righteous seeking the presence of the Holy but not only in a spiritual way. The book is intended to endow the practitioner with the same ability to ascend as that enjoyed by Ezekiel.

The Mishnah teaches this book is not to be shared with more than one student at any time (Hagigah 2:1). This prohibition is supported by a further regulation of access – that the student can understand the text with minimal direction. The teacher provides only the basic heading for the information, with the student doing the heavy lifting. This is to prevent the promiscuous transmission of information deemed "secret" and potentially dangerous. Praying ourselves into the presence of powerful angels and even that of the Holy One is not an evening with a Ouija board. It's serious business, so the writers of Ma'aseh Merkavah built something like a firewall around its potent contents to make that clear.

The reasoning was the danger of the journey itself, added to by the armies of angels who filled the seven palaces. On the way to the chariot of God, there was great peril. And so, Ma'aseh Merkavah aims to create a conduit for practitioners to arrive safely at the throne-chariot of the Holy One by prayer, which invoked the secret names. The book is both a guide and a protective amulet.

The extreme dedication required to attempt the journey is not for the faint of heart, and only those who have been fully educated and can understand the significance of the journey, following Ezekiel's visions, are encouraged to approach the throne-chariot.

The Introduction of Ecstasy

Preceding the introduction of Kabbalah, Ma'aseh Merkavah also informs it, introducing ecstasy as part and parcel of the mystical experience. Representing total union with God, both spiritually and physically, this concept becomes formative in Kabbalah and central to its aims. But it's also clear that the undertaking of such an ecstatic experience was closely guarded, as it presented practitioners with physical and spiritual danger.

Students were taught that by employing specific positions, they were more likely to see the throne-chariot. For example, some were taught to place their heads between their knees. For a vision to be ecstatic, the involvement of the body was necessary, as only in complete surrender of the whole student might the Holy precincts be seen.

This complete surrender and involvement of the physical and spiritual were carried forward into Kabbalah, in which that ecstasy is actively sought and embraced. This makes Ma'aseh Merkavah a template to the later formation of Kabbalah.

While clear that Ma'aseh Merkavah has its origins in the earliest layer of Jewish Mysticism as a school of theosophical thought and practice, like other mystical books, it's not considered part of Talmud. Rather, it is a companion who stands apart and in the specific canon of Jewish Mysticism - Kabbalah.

As we've just read, Jewish Mysticism is about a lot more than priestly political skirmishes. Jewish Mysticism, having its roots in the Bible, and having spawned a wealth of apocryphal literature outside the Hebrew canon of scripture, has endured due to the depth, beauty, and complexity of its practice but also because of its intrinsic connection to key moments in Jewish history. It stands as a spiritual salve to the turbulence, violence, and harassment suffered by the Jewish people as they've moved through history.

A Temple of the spirit for a people historically compelled to wander the world in search of safety and acceptance is the gift of Jewish Mysticism, handed down by these disenfranchised Temple priests, dissatisfied with legalism and the rigors of the Temple, its clerics and the political consequences of these. But there are many other gifts to be revealed as we continue our exploration of Jewish Mysticism. So, let's move on to the enormous and fascinating subject of Kabbalah, which will form the heart of this book.

I'll break the information offered into several chapters, ordered:

- Sefer Yetzirah, the history of Kabbalah's development and formative figures
- The Sefirot

- Concepts – Tzimtzum, Shevirah and Tikkun

- Linguistic mysticism and Gematria

- Zohar

The subject is huge, so I've organized the chapters about Kabbalah into easy to digest chunks, as there is probably no body of mystical knowledge quite so wide-ranging and variously influenced as Kabbalah.

I invite you on a layperson's journey into the mysteries of the Kabbalah, its history, texts, concepts, and points of interest for Jew and Gentile alike.

Chapter Three: The Kabbalah, a Work of Many Centuries and Many Hands

"They say you can't study Kabbalah until you are at least 40 years old. You know why? You have to have experienced at least one generation making the same mistakes as the previous one."

David Mamet

And it's true. The study of Kabbalah is traditionally limited to people over 40. This is the age of reason and experience. When you've reached it, you're most likely ready for what this canon of Jewish Mysticism offers. As a resident of the 21st Century, I need to admit that mileage may vary. A person of 40 years, these days, would seem much less equal to the intellectual and spiritual challenges offered by this literature than someone of earlier times. We seem to have become a little reluctant to "adult" in our day.

But the requirement for ID at the gate of Kabbalah is predicated on the layers attached to the Torah. These must be mastered by anyone approaching the study of these mystical texts.

These are:

- **Peshat:** The literal, plain meaning of the text. Without understanding this fundamental level of Torah, there's no point going on to the next, which is *remez* (meaning "hint").

- **Remez:** The remez is diving beneath the literal meaning of scripture to the hidden meaning just beneath the surface, which is only hinted at.

- **Drash:** Drash roughly equals exegesis, which is the use of other scriptures to interpret the one you're reading. Even if these sources are apocryphal, they're still considered illuminative and, thus, a formal component of Torah, hence the texts of midrash. The tale told is to be interpreted considering the Torah portion being read and not literally.

- **Sod:** This term refers to an esoteric reading of Torah, which illuminates the big questions, like why we're here and what the nature of the Divine is. The word "sod" means secret, so this level is the secret uncovered only by the faithful and spiritually realized student.

Another word for "sod" is "kabbalah," which translates as "received tradition."

Kabbalah – An Ancient Mystery

For all our efforts to historically pigeonhole Kabbalah, it resists, and that resistance is part of its ethereal, esoteric nature. Traditionally, Kabbalah is said to have originated in the Garden of Eden, being passed from Adam up through the generations of humanity via the righteous of God – the Tzadikkim.

Talmud, tractate Hagidah, counsels that Kabbalah should not be taught to those who are unprepared or haven't reached a level of wisdom by which they're able to absorb its lessons properly. By the time Kabbalah's blossoming in the Middle Ages, Kabbalah had traditionally become part of the Oral Torah, which was received by Moses at Sinai. So, perhaps in this latter claim, we find the origin of the prohibitions about the public and promiscuous transmission of Received Tradition.

As we read in the previous chapter, this prohibition began with the "firewalls" erected by Rabbis in the Geonic period, intended to signal the deeply esoteric, unknown nature of the spiritual and physical ecstasy sought in the ascent to the throne-chariot. Ma'aseh Merkavah, when physical and spiritual ecstasy was introduced as a means of ascent to union with God, became central to the practices and beliefs to emerge in Kabbalah.

Sefer Yetzirah

As you've been reading, I'm sure it's occurred to you how convoluted and multifarious the history of Jewish Mysticism is. That theme will continue in this chapter and those who follow.

Such is the nature of a movement that stands both within and outside the institutional Jewish Faith. But this is the story of most mystical movements in monotheistic systems. The Sufis hold a similar position in Islam, while Christian mysticism's long and varied history has also been marginalized.

But by the same token, interest in mysticism has given rise to endless interpretations and permutations of Jewish mystical texts and communities, many of them outside the tradition of Judaism.

But that's part of the adventure – following the threads of history and folklore to arrive at an enhanced understanding of what the Jewish mystics were building. That project has come down to us as a tremendous body of literature that continues to fascinate us.

The Sefer Yetzirah (Book of Formation) is considered the earliest book of Kabbalah. But even here, the tale is fraught with differences of scholarly opinion. Some date the book to the Middle Ages, while others date it to the Third or Fourth Centuries CE or the Second Century CE. And as this is not a scholarly work, we can accept the last of these.

While tradition attributes the book's authorship to Abraham, the more likely author is Rabbi Akiva ben Yosef (5o-135 CE), a leading contributor to Midrash and Mishnah. Some scholars believe he redacted earlier writings, whether Abraham or others authored them or passed them down orally. Folkloric accounts attribute the book to Adam, who transmitted it to Noah, who transmitted it to Abraham.

Throughout history, there have been several versions accepted of Sefer Yetzirah, as follows:

- A brief version of 1300 words

- A longer-form version of approximately 2600 words

- The version Saadia Gaon used to write his 10th Century commentary, called the "Saadia version"

- The Gra version of the Vilna Gaon (called "the Gra") used the version produced by Isaac Luria in the 16th Century to harmonize it with the Zohar, creating the 18th Century "Gra version"

As I've pointed out earlier in this book, the Sefer Yetzirah is difficult to pin down; while its themes concern Creation, it's also deeply concerned with language and numerals. The numerous redactions it's undergone have only muddied the waters.

No book in existence - not even the Torah or the combined Jewish and Christian scriptures of the modern Bible - has been so keenly examined. While the later Jewish Mystics held the book in great reverence, there are fundamental differences between this book and others in the canon of Kabbalah, especially about the sefirot, which we'll discuss in the next chapter. For example, the sefirot in this book don't correspond to those of later Kabbalistic writings.

In Sefer Yetzirah, there is a distinct indication of later ideas, especially in the repudiation of a Creation "from nothing." This follows the cosmology of Greek philosophy, of which Parmenides was the father in the 2nd Century BCE. Parmenides concluded that "ex nihilo nihil fit" (nothing comes from nothing). This appeared in the

Physics of Aristotle and was quoted throughout the world of the Ancient Greeks.

The model for Creation seen in Sefer Yetzirah posits the work of God in tandem with the universe. In this model, God is the "first mover" working with what the universe had, rather than the omnipotent architect of nothingness. This model was to be perpetuated throughout the Kabbalistic canon.

Sefer Yetzirah is a discussion of the 6 days of Creation from a mystical standpoint, including, in the first line, all the names of God. It then enlists the Divine numbers, including 7, 10, and 12. There is also a discussion of how the letters of the Hebrew alphabet were used in concert with the ten sefirot while engaged in Creation's work.

At the book's conclusion, God reveals the secret of Creation to Abraham, presenting it as an everlasting covenant between them. There were two aspects to this covenant, as described in the book:

- The covenant of circumcision (mila or "word") expressed on the human body between the ten toes on our feet.

- The covenant of the tongue (lashon) expressed as dwelling between the ten fingers on our hands. Lashon also refers to spoken/written language.

At the end of Sefer Yetzirah, God reveals the 22 letters of Torah to Abraham in the realization of the covenant of the tongue, unlocking the secrets of the Torah to him.

Linguistic Mysticism

The prominence of language in Sefer Yetzirah as a conduit for the Divine's work in Creation sets the stage for later Kabbalah. The book's viewpoint is that humanity and the Creation in which it's set result from various combinations of letters. Consider "Adam," the first man, and "Adamah," God's Creation. The significance is clear.

Key to the book's linguistic philosophy is the Hebrew letters aleph, mem, and shin (roughly corresponding to the English A, M, and S.) These letters stand as primordial maternal figures and the sources of the other letters in the aleph-bet. But Sefer Yetzirah takes that status further, framing the three as symbols of three corresponding primordial elements – air, fire, and water, re-visioning them as the sources which underlie all life.

Opposites in Unity

One of the strongest themes in the Sefer Yetzirah is that of the existence of pairs in both the physical and spiritual realms. The proposition is that these are continually at war – or in tension – but find unity in God.

Returning to aleph, mem, and shin and their correspondence to the three primordial elements, air, fire, and water, fire and water are held in tension and mediated by the presence of air. There are, according to Jewish Mysticism, seven of these warring pairs in human life:

- War and peace
- Wisdom and foolishness
- Life and death
- Poverty and wealth
- Servitude and rulership
- Ugliness and beauty

This theory of contrasting pairs corresponds to thinking in traditional Rabbinical Judaism. Yetzer ha-tov (urge to do good) and yetzer ha-ra (urge to do evil) exist in tension, and without the other, there is no coherence in human life or in Creation itself. For example, the Midrashic reference found in Genesis Rabbah 9:7. states that if it were not for yetzer ha-ra, there would be no ambition. People would stop working, building houses, and having children. This commentary refs directly to Torah's Genesis 1:31, in which "God saw everything that he had made and behold, it was very good."

The good resulting from a complete lack of evil in the world would not be what we think of "good" as being. Creation would be Stepford, in other words, *only more boring.* The human drive to succeed in the world is linked to our survival instinct, which is the urge to prevail over the elements, predators, and sometimes, other people. In that challenge is the meaning of the tension between the two urges in human nature.

Thus, God's mediating influence as Creator brings coherence to all life and mediation to all its opposing forces, making sense of them. Not only are these opposites held in tension, but neither exists without the other. All exist because of the tension these opposites are held in. Without death, would life be as sweet?

This frames humanity as a free agent, able to make choices about how to live and how to treat others.

The Development of Kabbalah

The philosophical orientation of Kabbalah is that of a prolonged examination and interpretation of the relationship between Ein Sof (The Infinite or without limit) and Creation.

Working within the framework of traditional Judaism and utilizing its Rabbinic texts to demonstrate the soundness of their mystical texts and beliefs, Kabbalah and its Miqqabal (Masters of Kabbalah) sought to reveal the secrets of the standing traditions of Judaism in its liturgies, practices, and writings.

Kabbalah, as we know it, did not emerge until the 12th and 13th Centuries in Southern France, enjoying a renaissance in 16th Century Palestine by the hand of Isaac Luria (1534 – 1572), born in Jerusalem.

Luria is one of Kabbalah's most renowned figures and, as such, is remembered as "Ha'ARI ("the Lion"). The Kabbalah we know today is Lurianic Kabbalah. While he wrote little himself, his oral traditions form the basis for Lurianic Kabbalah, having been transcribed by his students and handed down through successive generations. It is said that his spiritual power is what led to his veneration and acknowledgment as the Miqqabal of Miqqabals.

Luria's work was most richly expressed in the formation of Hassidic Judaism, which will be discussed later in this book. Formed in the 18th Century, it was in the Hassidic community that Kabbalah came to be most widely studied and disseminated.

Medieval Europe

The blossoming of Kabbalah in Medieval Europe began in the 12th Century, with the formation of private, secretive groups following a mystical impulse in Judaism. But the scholars locate the formation of Medieval Kabbalah in the southern French provinces of Languedoc and Provence.

Near the end of the 12th Century, Sefer ha Bahir appeared in this milieu, bearing an example of the sefirot. Closely identified with this book is Isaac the Blind (1160 - 1235). From southern France, Kabbalah was transmitted to northeastern Spain, where Nahmanides (1194 - 1270) emerged, advancing a Hellenistic interpretation of the sefirot, rooted in Neo-Platonism.

It was with the Castilian Miqqabals in the late 13th Century that Kabbalah produced the Zohar (the Book of Splendor), which was chiefly concerned with the unity of opposites, especially male/female attributes and the mediating influence between them of the Divine.

In this incarnation of Kabbalistic development, traditional Judaism and its Mystics were very much aligned, with material contributions coming from the Rabbinical Judaism of the day.

The Zohar stands as a central text in Kabbalah, and for the Jews of the day, it was Kabbalah itself. The publication of this key text birthed Kabbalah, which continued to flourish and reach its zenith with the establishment of Lurianic Kabbalah in 16th Century Palestine.

Comfort, Comfort, O My People

The history of Kabbalah is peppered with the tragedy of the incessant persecution of the Jewish people. This was no less true of Second Temple Jewish Mysticism than it was of 16th Century Lurianic Kabbalah.

European anti-Semitism in the Middle Ages was no less virulent than it was in the early to mid-20th Century, and this societal impulse played out across Europe in the Crusades, reaching an apogee in the 1492 Expulsion of the Jews from Spain. This concluded the flowering of Judaism in Spain and that of Medieval Kabbalah in its European setting.

Jews across Europe turned to their spirituality to weather their abuse at the hands of governments and gentile citizens, looking to the return of the Messiah for comfort. Part of that comfort was the historic homeland of Israel.

And so, Safed, the childhood home of Isaac Luria, became a center for international Jewry, including those who were mystics. From this cauldron of Jewish liturgical, legal, and Kabbalistic expression emerged, Moses Cordovero (1522 – 1570). Cordovero shifted the focus of Kabbalah to Jewish Messianic hope, to answer the cries of people living in exile and persecution, as Jews had lived in Babylon and under the boot of Rome in post-Second Temple Palestine. Popularizing the Zohar, he was part of a renaissance in the Judaism of the time, representing the very Messianic hope Jews were seeking.

And it was to be Cordovero that Isaac Luria took up the mantle of, arriving in an enlivened Safed in 1569.

Engrossed in the study of the Zohar at the tender age of 22, Luria became an aesthete, but he was married at 15, in Egypt, where a wealthy uncle supported him following the death of his parents. He is said to have lived in a hut on the Nile River, speaking not even to his family, who he visited only on the Sabbath.

In Safed, Luria taught, becoming incredibly influential as Cordovero had before him. Here, he expounded on Kabbalah, making the mystical branch of Judaism the most influential of the day, particularly about the liturgy.

Safed and Israel, generally, had seen a tremendous influx of Jews fleeing the Spanish Expulsion. Many gathered in the Galilee (where Safed is located) to await the return of the Messiah, a trend that had led Cordovero to re-orient Kabbalah toward Messianic Mysticism. But because Luria framed Kabbalah in the narrative of Exile, Jews found tremendous comfort in his teachings. And while Luria was not one to write his mysticism down, preferring to share a first-person pedagogy with students, his students recorded and disseminated his teachings. By the mid-1600s, his work was known by Jews in distant Europe – the birthplace of the canon of Kabbalah.

Largely responsible for this dissemination was a student of Luria's, Chaim Vital. He collected the transcriptions made of Luria's teachings. From these came the eight volumes of Etz Chaim (The Tree of Life), the basis of Lurianic Kabbalah, as derived from the Zohar.

Etz Chaim and Lurianic Kabbalah

It was Luria's work, via Vital, that made sense of the Zohar. Etz Chaim is a collection of "gates" describing prayers for every occasion presenting in Jewish daily, Sabbatical, and Festival life.

Vital was to record all Luria's teachings in a collection of books that form the Lurianic Kabbalah. These works are collectively known as the Kitvei Ari (The Writings of the Lion). Due to these works, the Zohar made sense and came to be intensively studied.

Etz Chaim is the cornerstone of a large body of writing. The "Gates" and their descriptions of prayers act as Kabbalistic illuminations, revealing the foundations of Kabbalistic thought.

The Pri Etz Chaim (Fruit of the Tree of Life) and Sha'ar Ha Kavanot (Gate of Meditations) are both dedicated to further illuminating Etz Chaim in terms of the practical application when preparing for prayer, for example, by ritually dressing in the prayer shawl and tefillim (phylacteries).

The Eight Gates

Building the Lurianic tradition continued with the production of the Shemonah Shearim (Eight Gates), named and instructing as follows:

- Sha'ar Hal lakdamot (Gate of Introductions). Much of the first of the Eight Gates books is a reiteration of Etz Chaim.

- Sha'ar Maamarel Rashbi (Gate of Zoharic Teachings of Rashbi, Rabbi Shimon Bar Yochai), which illuminates Zohar from the Second Century Rashbi's.standpoint. Considered highly revelatory as to the nature of Creation.

- Sha'ar Maamarel Chazal (Gate of Talmudic Teachings) as the book directly above, but illuminating the teachings of the sages, from the mystical standpoint.

- Sha'ar Ha Peskum (Gate of Biblical Verses), illuminating Torah as a spiritual, meditative journey into the lives of the ancestors.

- Sha'ar Ha Mitzvot (Gate of the Commandments), illuminating the ten Commandments as delivered to Moses at Sinai on a mystical basis.

- Sha'ar Ha Kavanot (Gate of Meditations) Describing the role of meditation in daily life and prayer in the first portion of the book and the second, Festivals and Shabbat, within a Kabbalistic framework

- Sha'ar Ruach Ha Kodesh (Gate of Divine Inspiration) Offering hundreds of meditations, the goal of this book is the perfection of the soul and the elevation of consciousness, with a prophetic bent.

• Sha'ar Ha Gilgulim (Gate of Reincarnations). This is a lengthy and complex treatment of reincarnation and how the soul must be perfected to return. The book also discusses the reincarnation of figures in the Bible.

These eight gates are theoretical, explained in practical terms by the Sha'ar Ruach Ha Kodesh. By reviewing each teaching of the Eight Gates, Ruach Ha Kodesh acts as a key to the full canon of Kitvei Ari, describing it as intensely meditative and prayerful. This is a key feature of a life centered on God and an awareness of God's presence in all things, from food to sex to interactions with other people.

The Eight Gates literature and Kitvei Ari contain the fullness of Isaac Luria, the Ari's, teachings and today; these writings are the most comprehensive canon of Kabbalah and the most compelling illuminative commentaries of the Zohar.

Isaac Luria revolutionized the world of Jewish Mysticism, shedding light where others had failed. Living to be only 38 years old, his brief stay on earth rendered incredible riches, popularizing Kabbalah and functionally legitimizing it in the tremendously complex world of Jewish literature.

But it wasn't until the 18th Century, when Hassidism arose in Ukraine as a spiritual revival movement, that Kabbalah was to be disseminated throughout the world. We'll talk about the Hassidim later in this book, as this is the community most responsible for the popularization of Jewish Mysticism. For the time being, we'll continue with our walk-through Kabbalah in the next chapter, in which we'll discuss the sefirot.

Chapter Four: The Sefirot - Emanations of the Divine

At the very heart of the Torah is the nishmata de'orayta - its inner soul. And that inner soul is expressed in the writings of Kabbalah. This is how Isaac Luria described the Kabbalah, not just linking it to Torah but defining it as the eternal spirit in which it was delivered to humanity.

Kabbalah, as Torah's hidden soul, bears prophecy and wisdom, foreseeing a transformed world in the revelation of Mashiach (the Messiah). The study of Kabbalah is the vehicle by which humanity is empowered to envision and give birth to that world, acting as midwives to the glory of a Creation transformed to fully reflect the glory of the Divine.

There is no greater expression of the eternal spirit in which the Torah was given as a gift to humanity than the sefirot. The sefirot stand as descriptive guides to the attributes which define an otherwise ineffable God.

These emanations or attributes work in concert with Creation, expressing the traits of God. As described in Sefer Yetzirah and elaborated on by Luria, the relationships between the sefirot are materialized, making them intelligible to those who study them.

The Tree of Life

The Torah, itself, is called the Tree of Life, and as the soul of the Torah, Kabbalah offers the sefirot organized into the shape of a type of tree, defining their relationships and manner of operating between one another and with Creation.

There are ten sefirot, named:

- Keter (Crown)

- Chokhmah (Wisdom)

- Binah (Understanding)

- Chesed (Lovingkindness)

- Gevurah (Might)

- Tiferet (Beauty)

- Hod (Splendour)

- Netzah (Victory)

- Yesod (Foundation)

- Shekhinah (Divine Presence), also called Malkhut (Sovereignty). NB: Shekhinah is a unique emanation, sited at the base of the Tree and thus, its root.

Each emanation expresses a trait of God. The Tree of Life scheme reveals the interdependence of all sefirot. But the truth about these emanations is that each contains all the others, expressing a certain internal "panentheism" – the idea that God infuses all things, as all things are in God. For the Tree of Life, God's emanations or traits are holistically unitive and cannot be separated from the whole. For example, with beauty comes judgment.

The Safed Kabbalists expounded on the concept of the interaction and interdependence of the sefirot, a clue to the disposition of Kabbalah in terms of the Creation it's illuminated. The panentheism of the Tree of Life in the internalized presence of all sefirot within each sefirah points to a Creation infused with God's Divine Presence and God's attributes living in every atom, every molecule, and every creature as they collective live in God.

Balance in the Tree of Life

Just as yetzer ha tov and yetzer ha rah are held in a mediating tension, so is the Tree of Life of the sefirot, expressing the balanced nature of God's Creation.

On the right side of the Tree are the attributes expressing unmitigated goodness in Chokhmah (Wisdom), Chesed (Lovingkindness), and Netzah (Victory). These are balanced by the attributes of the sefirot arranged on the opposite side, Binah (Understanding), Din (Judgment), and Hod (Splendor), expressing the fear and awe of the Divine. Without balance, these attributes – like yetzer ha rah – can easily run amok in Creation, and so, their activity is mitigated by the attributes on the right, which is sometimes called the "Pillar of Mercy."

Uniting the two sides of the Tree of Life is Tiferet (Beauty). This is the synthesis of the balance in which the sefirot exist. With Chesed defining the sefirot of the right side and Din defining those on the left, the balance expressed by Tiferet points to the balance in Creation, that of justice and mercy being necessary for the universe to operate as it was intended to.

At the bottom of the Tree, it's supported by Yesod (Foundation), providing stability, and underneath, in the fertile ground from which it grows, Shekhinah (the Divine Presence) which stands apart from the 10 Sefirot, being the active means of interaction with humanity and Creation and yet nourishing their activity. Through Shekhinah, the other sefirot are known.

In Tikkunei Zohar, a collection of hymns and part of its canon, the sefirot are described as how the unknowable Divine conceals its full glory from humanity. The sefirot, then, provide a means of not so much knowing God as approaching God's intentions via the emanations of Divine attributes. While not themselves, God, they tell us something about God.

Ein Sof

In Kabbalistic thought, God is the infinite, the limitless, the "without end." This understanding is taken from the description of Solomon ibn Gabirol (1021 - 1070), describing Ein Sof as "the endless one."

The Neoplatonic philosophy of God having no thoughts, words, actions, and desires is alive in this description of the Divine, which states we can't truly know what is without limit.

We'll talk much more about the Zohar after this series of chapters, but the description of Ein Sof in this book is instructive. Before the Creation of the universe, the Divine was formless, with no means of self-expression. Through Creation, God took on a veiled form in that work, revealing the true nature of Ein Sof through the emanations borne by the Sefirot.

For this reason, Zohar instructs that the name of God is too Holy to pronounce. It was only following the Creation of Adam, God's expression of Creation in the form of humanity, that God could descend, deploying Adam as a chariot. From this text comes the tetragrammaton - yud hey vav hey - YHVH.

The philosophy of the Tetragrammaton further reveals the reasoning behind the term. Formulated by Jewish Mystics of the Middle Ages, the concept advanced is that only that which has limits may be named. This concept can also be found in the Creation narrative of Genesis when God named the sun and moon. These are named the "greater light to rule the day and the lesser light to rule the night - and the stars" (Genesis 1: 16).

In the historical context, this verse was written in, the sun and moon were worshipped in the Pagan World, so the intention is clear. By naming them as no more than the providers of light, God has removed their divine power. What is named is limited. What is not named is limitless and beyond all other powers in existence. And what flows from that limitless, ineffable source is the Ohr Ein Sof (the light of the limitless), as expressed in the sefirot and their revelation of the nature of God. This is the true Divine light.

Ayin

Ayin existed before Ein Sof's revelation in Creation, but that nothingness is as complex and unknowable as Ein Sof itself. Ineffable, it is named by the Mystics "I am becoming," expressing a reality both being born and unborn – a nothing on its way to being something.

At the nexus of nothingness and birth is the faith required to understand, on some level, if never fully, that nothingness is a kind of existence, an existence that, while never being born, is eternally in labor.

In terms of Jewish Mysticism, Ayin is the transcendence of being while representing a mode of existence beyond human understanding. So, from the singular state of becoming that is not being but something set apart therefrom, comes Ein Sof.

And Ein Sof, the limitless, ineffable Divine, communicates its nature through the sefirot in the Tree of Life. Next, let's examine the ten sefirot individually, besides Shekhinah, the root of the Tree.

Keter (Crown)

Sometimes called "Keter Elyon" (Crown of the Most High), this sefirah refers to the initiative of God rising. This initiative or Will exists even before any cognitive recognition.

Emanating from the Ayin, the limitlessness of Ein Sof is expressed as a tangible symbol, signifying the crowning of the Kabbalistic student through the death of the ego. This is the achievement of unity with God, sought through the mediating sefirot and their expository illumination of the Divine attributes.

Associated with Keter is the name of God revealed in the burning bush narrative (Exodus 3: 1-21). When, in verse 13, Moses asks God for a name to share with the exiled Israelites in Egypt, God responds: "Ehyeh asher ehyeh" - "I will be what I will be." And so, the name is "Ehyeh," meaning "by my will I will become as I choose to become," again ineffable and imminently limitless by the Divine's self-definition, at least in this verse. As the "crown," the Keter is immaterial, representing knowledge to come through the Divine revelation of God's attributes.

Chokhmah (Wisdom)

This sefirah represents the creative impulse and the primordial Torah - the purest form of Divine wisdom. Analogous to intuition, which, without reason, doesn't equate to "thought" but is driven by the same physical processes as instinct, the sefirah may be described as the Divine inspiration to form Creation.

Chokhmah is also conceptualized as a sperm that plants itself in Binah (Understanding) to initiate the process of Creation. This is not a "sexed" action, as Ein Sof, having no body, does not have a sex, either. Rather, Ein Sof expresses both the male and female - and neither.

Associated with Chokhmah is the name "Yah," which is the yud in the Tetragrammaton - YHVH. The significance of yud can be approached by understanding that some Jews will use only the yud hey portion of the Tetragrammaton to express God's name in written texts and some, only the yud. Others will express the name of God with a point due to its Holiness and power.

Binah (Understanding)

It's in this sefirah that the creative process becomes material. Binah is the womb receiving the sperm of Chokhmah, giving birth to the other seven sefirot in the Tree. Binah may be described as discernment, which is a function of thought. It's here that the intuition of Chokhmah becomes guided by the conscious act of thought.

Binah may be thought of as a mother, to Chokhmah's father role, building from the spark of Divine inspiration all the other sefirot acting as created emissaries of the traits of the unknowable God.

The name of God associated with Binah is "Elohim," or the heavenly hosts. It's a plural word used throughout the Bible as God's name, with the implication that while God is One, the Divine ineffable encompasses all within it, thus integrating representations of deity that existed before the establishment of monotheism. But also reflected in the name Elohim is the historical reality of how Judaism developed in the Ancient Near East.

In its earliest layer, Judaism cleaved to a henotheistic worldview (one God among many). This was revised to monotheism over time, beginning in the 6th to 7th Century BCE and continuing through Babylonian Exile.

Chesed (Lovingkindness)

Chesed is the unlimited love of the Divine. Unconditional and unstinting, this is the love we all desire as humans. Chesed may also be translated as "compassion," but lovingkindness is the preferred translation.

There is an extravagance in the lovingkindness of God, which is to be expected considering that the source is without end. This attribute of God is primary, preceding all others. Unprovoked, it is rained down upon Creation "just because."

On Chesed, Creation is founded, and in that foundation, lovingkindness is limitlessly supplied, unprovoked and abundant.

This sefirah is linked to the Divine name El (God) or El Elyon (the Most High). The Hebrew word "El" in pre-monotheism describes any god. This is evidenced in the name "El Elyon," which translates as the "highest god," reflecting Judaism's early henotheism.

Gevurah (Might)

Gevurah stands in tension with Chesed. While fundamentalists of all stripes cleave to Gevurah and the judgment and punishment it signifies, without the balance of Chesed (which is freely given to all beings and not only the righteous), humanity and the Creation it inhabits would buckle under the weight of Gevurah.

And without Gevurah? Creation would be absorbed and return to the Ayin with Ein Sof, itself. The reality of this balance between lovingkindness and might/judgment is that it's a common theme in all Jewish literature, including the Talmud, Midrash, and Tanakh (the written Torah). Because in balance is the integrity of the Tree itself and that of Creation. This is one of the most important features of the architecture of the Tree and a sustaining truth about the nature of God and God's Creation.

The name associated with Gevurah is again, Elohim.

Tiferet (Beauty)

Further balancing the tension between Chesed and Gevurah is the sefirah at the Tree's center – Tiferet. Also called "glory," Tiferet serves as an additional balance to ensure the functionality of the universe and all it encompasses.

This sefirah is unitive, bringing together the nine upper attributes and considered the primary attribute. Some Trees of Life name Tiferet Rachamim (Mercy). The root of the word Rachamim is also instructive, as it's the same as that of the word "womb" (Rachem).

And so, right in the middle of the Tree of Life is a womb which unifies the other sefirot to unify God's attributes and, thus, Creation. At the same time, this womb gives birth to the beauty which serves as one of the Divine's most compelling traits.

The Tetragrammatom (YHVH) is the name most associated with Tiferet, and the letter "vav."

Netzah (Victory) and Hod (Splendor)

Like the interaction and tension between Chesed and Gevurah, Netzah and Hod are "codependent" sefirot. Their emanations are more focused on the material world than the spiritual world, though, which is an important distinction. Netzah's victory is that of God's work in Creation, as primarily composed of grace and love of what has been created. Hod describes God's judgment and how it's administered. Hod also describes prophecy and its power to unite, indict, and move humanity.

The name associated with these two sefirot is YHVH Tsva'of (the Lord of Hosts) but also Elohim Tsva'of (God/gods of hosts). The energetic exchange between these two sefirot as attributes of God is a tension without which imbalance would occur. Fiery judgment and equally fiery prophecy prevent an annihilating love fest and the total collapse of Creation into its source.

Yesod (Foundation)

Yesod is the Foundation but also the reproductive force of nature in Creation, embodied in the fertility of all creatures and encompassing crops and other plant life. Uniting the two pillars on either side of the Tree of Life, directly beneath Tiferet, this sefirah appears above Shekhinah/Malkhut providing a conduit between the Tree's central womb and the creative potential of Shekhinah/Malkhut, facilitating fecundity by flooding it with life on the edge of being born.

Yesod, then, is symbolized by the male member and is closely associated with the Jewish rite of circumcision, the sign of belonging, and the mitzvah (commandment or blessed deed), which brings male Jews under the umbrella of Jewish belonging.

Yesod is associated with the name of God, El-Hai (the Living God) and El Shaddai (God Almighty/God of the Mountains).

Shekhinah (the Divine Presence)/Malkhut (Sovereignty)

At the base of the tree is the Divine Presence, popularly known as Shekinah. All the other sefirot are synthesized in this emanation, which is the human experience of God, beyond all intellectual exercises but known in the believer's heart and soul.

With Ein Sof as sovereign God, humanity knows God's presence and qualities through the agency of Shekhinah/Malkhut. In times of exile, Shekhinah goes with the Jewish people. And when all wanderings cease with the revelation of the Meshiach, so will Shekhinah stop in her wanderings.

Shekhinah/Malkhut is associated with God's name, Adonai (Our Lord – reflecting God's sovereignty over Creation).

As in Heaven, so on Earth

The balanced nature of the Tree of Life expressed in the sefirot reflects humanity's role of steward to Creation. Our understanding of the Divine emanations as expressed in them realizes their purpose, which is communicative and eschatological (defining Creation's purpose and the eschaton which will eventually bring it into an unhindered and unblemished relationship with its Creator).

What we do here, as humans, impacts the heavens. This instruction is found in the Christian scriptures, as uttered by the Nazarene Jew, Jesus, in Matthew 18:18, who said that what we "bind on earth will be bound in heaven" and what we "loose on earth will be loosed in heaven" (Matthew 18:18).

This concept of synchronized consequences for human actions is the problem the sefirot are here to help us solve. In its balance between judgment and lovingkindness, victory and splendor, the Tree of Life formed by the sefirot is a guidebook for human activity. The injunction is clear – that we, in our actions, echo that balance to ensure that the life of Heaven and life on earth are operating in tandem and harmony.

It's when that balance is achieved that God's unity with humanity can occur, provoking the revelation of the Messiah. And that balance and unity can only occur, following the assertions of the Jewish Mystics, by the fervent application of prayer, meditation, fulfilling the mitzvot and the mastery of a soul turned toward the Divine.

In the sefirot, we see a thumbnail of the traditional texts of Judaism. Encapsulated in perfect balance, they form a picture not only of what God is "like" but of what we have the potential to be and to achieve via worship, study, righteous living, and righteous action, by way of mitzvot.

In our next chapter, we'll talk about the world of the sefirot in terms of the concepts of tzimtzum, shevirah, and tikkun.

Chapter Five: Tzimtzum, Shevirah and Tikkun

As we've read in the previous chapter, the Tree of Life provides us with a means of understanding God's attributes and how they work in Creation. We've learned of the balance and harmony they represent. Looking at and studying the Tree, we come to find that while God is known in Creation, the sefirot help us apprehend a deeper level of understanding, acting as our guides.

But the sefirot also have an intensely dramatic story to share about how Creation came to be, in the concepts of tzimtzum, shevirah, and tikkun.

Tzimtzum

Understanding the beginning of the process by which Creation was inspired was the gradual emergence of Ein Sof from the "becoming" state of Ayin (a nothing that is something). In tzimtzum, the Divine Will enacts a unique strategy in which "space" is made for Creation and all its creatures.

Some Kabbalistic texts have portrayed tzimtzum as a gradual contraction of the Divine to make this possible. But Isaac Luria saw this very differently. He contended that Ein Sof's concealment via contraction was sudden. In Luria's mind, Ein Sof transformed the function of deity in this instance from "limitless" to "limited."

The literal meaning of tzimtzum is "contraction," but this contraction also posits a transformation. The Ohr Ein Sof (light of the limitless), as explained in the Etz Chaim of Chaim Vital, is a manifestation of Divine Power but taking on the ethereal properties of light, which is transient and impermanent. For Creation to be accomplished, Ohr Ein Sof needed to be concealed or transformed, subsuming the infinite for the finite.

The rays of the sun offer a worthy analogy. As the greater light of the sun shines upon us, the ray of sun is indistinct. It has no individuality but is part of the sun's light and warmth. Far away from the sun, when observed as what it is - "a ray of sun," it becomes uniquely what it is: "a ray of sun." In the same way, the Ohr Ein Sof, observed, is a finite manifestation of the great light of the Endless One.

Another fitting analogy is that of Einstein "removing" or "contracting" his knowledge of Quantum Physics to teach his students basic mathematics. For the sake of revelation and for the students to be able to ascend to higher levels of mathematical understanding, he cordoned off this knowledge to create a firm foundation. This is much like the process of tzimtzum.

For the sake of revelation in the Created order, Ein Sof limited its limitlessness.

What tzimtzum means is that Ein Sof not only contracted and concealed itself to perform the act of Creation but emanated into that Creation as a natural element. This transformation represents no change in the nature of God. God does not change. As stated in Malachi, "I, God, do not change" (Malachi 3:6). Without changing,

God temporarily creates space in the concept of tzimtzum, almost as though taking on a disguise.

The God of Creation is the same today, aloof and yet immanent in the stuff of Creation. The change was in the act of Creation itself, which is a revelation of Divine Power and a manifestation of its eternality, as accomplished through the Ohr Ein Sof.

Reshimu

After tzimtzum, there remained a "residue," akin to what might be left in an empty olive oil bottle. In Hassidism, this residue is explained as a series of letters. This is the literal translation of the word "reshimu" – "letters of the residue."

In essence, Ein Sof's act of Creation was first assessed as an inspiration, with the letters of the residue representing the formation of Divine Will before tzimtzum. These explain the potential for the self-limitation represented by Ohr Ein Sof.

"Definition" is a keyword here, with the reshimu providing it through the vehicle of language. In Kabbalah, letters build the words which convey meaning and are called kelim (vessels). Through the kelim, we arrive at the meaning of the words formed, which is the Ohr (light).

Tzimtzum gave birth to the Kelim which only existed as concepts before Creation. Infused with Ohr Ein Sof, they were the agents of definition, representing the possibility of concealment/contraction. In tzimtzum, the reshimu were drained of Ohr Ein Sof, making the limitation of Ein Sof possible through their defining, boundary-building agency.

Reshimu might also be explained as "memory." We remember certain key events in our lives, but we can't relive them. We remember the taste of wine after we've consumed it. The taste remains in our mouths when the wine has been drunk. These memories and traces are comparable to the traces of the Endless Ones we approach through the texts of the Kabbalah.

The Four Worlds

Kabbalah posits a four-stage Creation process, described as four worlds. To start, the stages of the creative process for a building project might look something like this:

- Inspiration/concept

- Concept development

- Planning

- Building

And the four worlds represent the biggest building project of all time – that of Creation. Each corresponds to a building project stage, and each stage has a corresponding sefirah or a group of sefirot.

Atzilut (Inspiration/Concept)

In this world, the sefirot are manifested. The name for this world – Atzilut – is derived from the root "aitzel," or "next to." It may also be interpreted as "emanating from." This is the world realized immediately after the Ohr Ein Sof contracts, through the act of tzimtzum.

In this first world, created in the aftermath of tzimtzum, finite Creation is born. Drained of Ohr Ein Sof, the Kelim or vessels are deployed to define the nature of God.

But Atzilut is still within the realm of the Limitless, which reflects on the nature of the sefirot. Bearing the Endless One's names, they are also infinite in scope and character, as emanations of God's traits. In Atzilut, each sefirah is revealed as distinct. While interacting with and bearing within them all the others, they are delineated as autonomous.

Chokhmah corresponds to this world, which is the potential of Creation.

Beriah (Concept Development)

In this world, potential takes shape as the concept of Creation is further developed. Not yet created, physically, a plan is coming together. The word Beriah explicitly means "creation." This is where the creative process breaks free, becoming its own thing.

Beriah is also called the "Divine Throne" (Kisei Hakavod). The idea is that God has descended to sit, contacting the tangible in the creative process. Because Beriah is that process approaching the tangible as an independent concept, God is sitting among the worlds.

The Angels and souls are created in the world of Beriah. These are the seraphim, from the root seraiphah (fire). Through their agency, the energetic requirements of Creation are met. The fiery seraphim are those most closely in contact with Ein Sof, burning with the intensity of the relationship.

The sefirah Binah corresponds to this world.

Yetzirah (Planning)

Yetzirah, which means "formation," is where the plans are finalized for what will become Creation. This is where ownership of the building project is taken, as it draws closer to material reality.

Yetzirah is the home of the "holy beings"; the chayot ha kodesh. These are the archangels Michael, Gabriel, and Raphael, and each is associated with a corresponding sefirah. Raphael to Tiferet, Michael to Chesed, and Gabriel to Gevurah. The holy beings in the world of Yetzirah operate in conjunction with the properties of these emanations. Again, through the agency of the Angels, the Divine traits infuse and inform Creation. As it's planned, these emanations are woven into the complexity of the work at hand.

This world corresponds with the 6 "emotional" sefirot from Chesed through Yesod.

Assiyah (Building)

Assiyah is where the action takes place. The inspiration has moved through the planning stages and is coming to fruition in this world.

Flowing through the conduits created by the Archangels of Yetzirah, Creation's 4 kingdoms are created in human, mineral, vegetable, and animal form.

In the world of Assiyah is a fascinating paradox. As Creation is being formed in all the diverse majesty and beauty, its Creator has contracted and is working in the purpose-built vacuum to conceal tzimtzum, the source of it all.

Ein Sof is hidden from what has been created through that Divine Will, to where Creation is ignorant of its source. But what's interesting is that the result is free will. Humanity is not compelled to acknowledge the presence of the Creator. A knowledge of God is, due to tzimtzum, a matter of personal agency. So concealed, the Divine invites us to seek its hiding place.

In the world of Assiyah, there is a profound challenge for humanity. As it materializes, the choice to seek God's hiding place is revealed as its true purpose. In concealment, God has built a home for his creatures, and in Assiyah, a challenge is issued to set about discovering where all this might have come from.

The sefirah associated with Assiyah is Shekhinah/Malkhut. From the standpoint of Shekhinah, Creation's materialization in its Divine construction is infused, in every molecule with all the attributes of God and this final world, with the Divine Presence. From the standpoint of malkhut, God as Sovereign, creating and reigning over Creation in concealment, is distant and yet immanent through the emanations and the agency of Angels.

Assiyah is the autonomy of Creation and the challenge of free will. But the Sovereign God in the self-exile of tzimtzum has issued an explicit invitation to play "hide and seek" to those willing to "play."

Shevirah

In 1570, Isaac Luria introduced the concept of shevirah into the canon of Kabbalah. Called shevirat ha kelim (the breaking of the vessels), in which the ten sefirot are depicted as vessels that can no longer contain the light of Holiness. In response to this intense pressure, they shatter, and the process of Creation is initiated.

This shattering takes place in the void (ayin), which is referred to in this model as "tohu" (chaos). Luria's parallel treatment of the Creation narrative in the shevirat ha kelim was drawn from close study and interpretation of the Zohar.

The shattering of the sefirot in shevirah distributes the shards of the kelim throughout the universe. But the model speaks directly to the brokenness of historic Judaism. Moses' shattering of the ten commandments on Mt. Sinai is just one example, with the destruction of the two Temples also standing as pivotal moments. This brokenness is echoed in the shevirah, which is a primordial preview of history yet to be written in Lurianic terms.

A theory in Kabbalah interprets the shevirah as not just a response to the pressure of containing the Ohr Ein Sof, but to instability in the nature of the light contained. The theory states that the kelim contained the light of evil and goodness and could no longer be contained. This depicts the breaking of the vessels as an act of purification, cleansing of Divinity. This theory has support in Torah, specifically in Isaiah 45:7, in which God reveals, "I form the light and create darkness: I make peace and create evil. I, the LORD, do all these things".

Let's return to the breaking of the ten commandments for a moment. Moses broke these due to his frustration with the Israelites. Having created the Golden Calf as a kind of visual aid, they had broken the Covenant through the Commandments by making an idolatrous representation. But God wasn't done with Moses, nor Moses with the intractable Israelites. He returned to Mt. Sinai and was graced with a second set of tablets. These were placed with the broken ones inside the Ark of the Covenant and carried with the people as they made their way to the Promised Land.

In this narrative is a truth that strikingly corresponds to the shevirah. Following the interpretation of shevirah ha kelim as a purification from evil in the Divine attributes, we must ask where that evil went? Well, nowhere!

Tohu, as chaos, is eternal, and the evil dispersed is eternal. Exodus's narratives tell us that life has its moments of shattering and those of redemption, and these must both be carried with us to honor that tension. Again, balance is the message. Human lives are not intended to be free of brokenness. Rather, they're to be defined by both brokenness and wholeness, failure and triumph, sadness and happiness. And this is God's presence as defined by the shevirah – everything can't be sunshine and lollipops all the time. Evil is always with us, and our relationship to it, while not always a matter of free will, is ours to explore and define. By carrying our brokenness with us as proudly as we carry our wholeness, we are fully human and entirely present to the reality of life.

Shevirah, then, while describing an event of shattering, holds within it the last of the concepts we'll discuss in this chapter – tikkun – the repair. Creation, due to shevirah, is not just a choice and a challenge. It's a covenant on its own, held with the entire Created Order. Those broken shards are ours to find and to return to their eternal source. This is how Creation is healed – with tikkun olam "the repair of the world."

Tikkun

While the concept of tikkun olam has taken on enormous popular currency through the avenue of Reform Judaism, the Lurianic interpretation is much more spiritually oriented. While the popular interpretation compels activism and community support – both of which may be "healing" – the Lurianic viewpoint is about spiritual healing and peace in the Created Order, through the reconstruction of the kelim.

The Hassidic Jewish community is the most potent proponent of the latter viewpoint, which seeks the Divine Presence through otherwise mundane acts. In food and other daily needs and practices, this Presence is acknowledged and served by ordering the material world to respond to the perceived desires of God. By living each day in service to God in every action taken, the Hassidim are performing tikkun.

So, while the popular perception of tikkun olam is to repair the material Created Order, Jewish Mysticism sees the process as a spiritual one – repairing the world from within each living soul. In the repair of the soul and its relationship to its Divine source is the true, holistic healing of the Created Order.

Isaac Luria's treatment of tikkun is complex. His model posits that the work of tikkun was accomplished in creating Primordial Man – Adam. But that is not how the story unfolded, as readers will be aware.

The story you most likely are unaware of is that Adam needed only to follow the Divine's contemplative instruction to accomplish tikkun. Uniquely placed in the Garden of Eden, Creation's very apex, he had everything he needed to do it.

Instead, he reached for that apple and took a bite. This single action created a butterfly effect, undoing the work of tikkun already accomplished. And why? Because the purification of the divine light had been undone. Once again, goodness blended with evil, and the Created Order was as muddled as the tohu from which it emanated.

Following Luria, the work of tikkun is an ongoing and urgent matter due to the action of Primordial Man. So, Adam's fall provoked the ongoing gathering of the kelim's shards, broken in shevirah ha kelim, and the gathering of the light in the souls of humans toward the spiritual repair of Creation.

Luria saw the shattering as a two-fold catastrophe – one in the Divine realm – shevirot ha kelim and one, in the realm of the human soul – sin. To repair the first, action on the part of humanity is required, and that action is to cleave to Holiness. As I stated earlier, the Hassidim (which will be discussed in the next section of this book) set themselves apart in response to Luria's interpretation of the Created Order as a locus of spiritual pollution.

But this idea was not novel in Luria's time. It comes down through history through an ancient source - Jewish Gnosticism. Arising in the First Century, this school of thought believed that knowledge of God represented salvation, but they believe this knowledge could only be obtained through a direct revelation. Further, the Gnostics repudiated the material world as intrinsically evil. While the treatment of evil in Lurianic Kabbalah is much more complex and perhaps less spiritualized than that of Gnosticism, there is an echo of this thinking in the Hassidic approach to living in the world.

And that approach is in keeping with the Lurianic concept of the material as containing evil, which must be purged from Creation. And this is the key point of departure in the tikkun of Lurianic Kabbalah and that of popularized tikkun. While popularized tikkun seeks to repair the world itself, Lurianic tikkun is focused on the spiritual world and the re-established perfection of Creation. It seeks not to repair this world but the next.

Thus, the olam ha tikkun (the world of repair) is a Creation purged of spiritual pollution, having repaired the problems of the Sin of Adam and the shevirot ha kelim, bringing with that restoration the coming of the Messiah.

Olam ha tikkun is the legacy of humanity. Having dropped the ball at a crucial moment, humanity is now charged with the stewardship of the Created Order (following the Divine commission in the Garden of Eden) as a cleanup crew. The Divine awaits the return of the shattered pieces of the sefirot and the restoration of Creation's transcendent spotlessness. But this may be achieved only through the ardent spiritual discipline of humans.

In our next chapter on the Kabbalah, we'll examine the traditions of linguistic mysticism and gematria and their place in Jewish Mysticism.

Chapter Six: Linguistic Mysticism and Gematria

Mysticism is a largely misunderstood component of religious belief. Some call it insanity, others delusion. But they might feel differently if they knew that the linguistic mysticism found in the canon of Kabbalah is how Natural Language Processing (NLP) in Artificial Intelligence got its start.

Focusing on communication between humans and machines, most believe Alan Turing (1912 – 1954) to be the father of NLP, in his assertion that computer-generated intelligence could coherently interact with humans. But Turing, for all his brilliant contributions to the field, was light years behind.

The locus classicus of NLP can be found in the quill of Abraham Abulafia (1240 – circa 1291) in Spain. Abulafia's practice was to write letters of the Hebrew alphabet, combining them in various ways. While the process might have appeared random to anyone watching him scribble away, his was a distinct system he called a science.

Discovered during his study of the Sefer Yetzirah, Abulafia was employing a secret rulebook from the pages of this Kabbalistic text. This text describes Creation as having been formed by combining the letters of the Hebrew alphabet. Abulafia's intense study of Sefer

Yetzirah concluded that the symbols of language could be transformed by applying the rules revealed in its pages, arriving at statements that further illuminated the original text.

In this manner, Abulafia wrote the books of the Prophetic Kabbalah, spending months combining all 22 letters of the alphabet to arrive at the actual texts. He claimed that the books, because of the methodology he'd used, were infused with the wisdom of the Biblical Prophets.

But not everyone agreed, and part of the reason for that disagreement is the tale of the Golem. For our purposes here, the Golem was an inanimate creation of a variety of Rabbi through applying the formulas set out in Sefer Yetzirah. In some of these tales of forbidden creative activity taken by humans – effectively standing in the place of the Almighty – this Golem turned on the Rabbi. In others, the Golem acted as a servant. Some Rabbis were said to have created livestock to eat. But there is a clear strain in Hassidim warning against creating living creatures, especially in the most famous of the tales, which takes place in Prague.

While rudimentary, this feature of linguistic mysticism is very similar to NLP, underscoring the complexity of thought poured into the production of Kabbalistic texts over many centuries. Jewish Mysticism is anything but simple-minded and, verges on genius in its constructs and explorations of language and numbers.

The Divine Word

The idea that language has great power is embedded in the Bible, particularly in the Creation narrative. Earlier in this book, I discussed the sun and moon's naming, reducing them to functions in the context of Creation, where Pagans had worshipped them as gods.

But that the Creation narrative depicts God as taking creative action through the power of language is a much more salient point in our discussion of linguistic mysticism. Throughout the Bible, it's clarified that "words matter." Words are creative, active, and almost material in their power.

Traditional Judaism is deeply invested in the holiness of the Hebrew language due to using God's direct Word in instigating the Created Order. In Sefer Yetzirah, Creation is accomplished via the deployment of the alphabet and that of the ten cardinal numbers (which we'll talk about a little later in this chapter, under the heading "gematria").

Going back to the sun and moon being put in their place as functionaries of the Created Order, it's important to note that Jewish Mysticism draws a direct link between the names of things and the thing itself. This is the power of naming and the power of the word in the narrative – it strips the sun and moon of their former status as deities, bringing them under the authority of the One Sovereign God.

What's in a Name?

For example, the earliest layer of the Kabbalistic canon, Sefer ha Bahir and Sefer Yetzirah, contains many lists of Angels and God's names, coupled with interpretations. In 13th Century Spain, these were closely studied and accompanied by the formulation of numeric equations, following Tanakh. The purpose of this was to interpret the Hebrew Scriptures by interpreting names and the clues provided by a number being assigned to every letter. Some practitioners used these formulas and interpretations to influence the Heavenly realms. But mystics like Abraham Abulafia, with his early NLP, believed that the divine names were the key to unlocking the deepest secrets to be found across the entire canon of Jewish literature. He believed that the system described in Sefer Yetzirah could bring the ardent practitioner into a state of unification with God.

The Cornerstone of Tikkun

It's in the destruction of the First and Second Temples that we find an impetus for the reification of language in Jewish Mysticism, as brilliantly explained by scholar Moshe Idel. The materializing of language created a means by which Judaism could construct that indestructible Temple we were contemplating earlier in this book.

Through applying fervent prayer, the performance of the mitzvot, and the study of the Torah, it was posited that a spiritual Temple could be built. In each prayer is the cornerstone of the Jewish Faith, rebuilding the Temple stone by stone – or word by word, letter by letter.

The prayers of the faithful replaced the Temple's ritual sacrifices. In tandem with being on the shevirot ha kelim cleanup crew, these linguistic actions and the spirituality associated with them are stewardship expressly commanded by God as the basis for tikkun. The Divine will make the Word, had built Creation. In return, humanity is enjoined to rebuild it through these spiritual disciplines.

In Jewish mystical thought, words are stones laid on top of one another until a perfected Creation, fully healed, arises. And prayer is the cornerstone of that effort. But it is the language from which prayer is created that is most important. Symbolism and the object connected to it are how language has the potential, when deployed ritualistically, to impact the Divine realm.

This belief is fundamental to Hassidism (especially in the 18th Century), primarily expressed via Lurianic Kabbalah and in the Zohar. Generally, Jewish Mysticism adheres to the belief that language is a material entity that builds a bridge between humanity and God in its reconstitution of the ancient Temple.

Sefer Yetzirah and Linguistic Mysticism in Creation

In Sefer Yetzirah, the letters of the Hebrew alphabet are much more than emissaries of the Divine creative force. They also stand as representatives of the Created Order. Held in the Hebrew language is Creation, and in Creation is held the Hebrew language.

This is the text which so influenced Abraham Abulafia in his production of the Prophetic Kabbalah. The alphabet is formed in the second sefirah (Chokhmah, "wisdom"). The narrative depicts God as then combining the 22 letters in every conceivable way as part of the act of Creation. The freedom inherent in using the letters, which falls outside the traditional canon of Jewish writings, is that of the Divine and the Divine alone.

Language, in Sefer Yetzirah, takes on cosmic significance. Specifically, the Hebrew language is cast as God's own, infusing Creation with the Divine word that brought it into being.

The Heikhalot Literature

The ancient texts of the Merkavah tradition further underscore the importance of language to the Jewish mystics. In Heikhalot literature, God's name is portrayed as intrinsic, with the Tetragrammaton and God described as consubstantial (of one substance).

The Heikhalot further describes every letter of the alphabet as a name of God, on its own. This idea reverberates through Kabbalistic traditions, particularly in Sefer Yetzirah, with the alphabet implicated in Creation itself. So, in its earliest layer, the canon depicts the letters of the Hebrew alphabet as having Divine agency but also as a link between God and humanity, inherent in Creation.

In this schema, the letters of the alphabet's energetic qualities provoked Creation's coming into being, as the Creator spoke them.

Graphics and Kabbalah

Kabbalah is also concerned with the Hebrew characters' graphic depiction, as these stand as the sefirot symbols. A change in their shapes would be considered a heretical act, as this would distort the image of God.

So, spoken or written, the significance of the Hebrew alphabet in Jewish Mysticism goes well beyond what is being conveyed in the text or any interpretations thereof. Via the forms of the letter – and to the Kabbalists, the white space around them – meaning is conveyed, thus shrinking the distance between the symbol and what it symbolizes. The letters themselves become Holy icons. Approaching Jewish religious literature's fullness with this in mind is central to understanding the mystical experience of language embodied by Kabbalah.

Sefer ha Temunah (the Book of the Image, late 13th Century) is a prolonged description and interpretation of Hebrew characters' mystical status, presenting them as symbols of the sefirot. But this book is not alone in its efforts to reify the Hebrew alphabet. It's accompanied by others in a similar vein. Sod Shem ha Meforash (the Secret of the Tetragrammaton) is assumed to have been produced by the same author, although attribution is muddy.

The tradition of gematria accompanies the tradition of linguistic mysticism. This system, which assigned numeric values to the alphabet, serves as an interpretative tool, adding another layer of meaning to the study of Holy literature.

Gematria

Derived from the Hellenistic (Greek) theory of numbers (esopsephy), gematria assigns a numeric value to letters. Using this model, readers can add the values of the letters to arrive at the numeric value of a word. This provides a means of interpretation in which spiritual significance can be detected through the word's numeric value.

Sources in Mishnah date the practice to Tannaic times, with Classical Hassidism being gematria's greatest proponent.

Guided by the Mispar, of which there are two versions – the hechrechi (absolute value) and gadol (larger value) – characters are assigned a value of 1 to 9, at the start of the alphabet (aleph through tet), then from 10 to 90 (yud through tzady). The next set of characters is assigned values from 100 to 400 (kuf through taf). The final characters, which are those used to end words (i.e., mem sofit), are also expressed in multiples of 100, from 500 through 900 (kaf sofit through tzady sofit) but only by the Mispar gadol. Mispar hechrechi doesn't assign a value to the sofit versions of the letters.

In Hebrew, vowels are expressed as pointings (although these are not always used) and aren't usually assigned a numeric value.

There are numerous mispar but describing them all would go well beyond the scope of this humble book, so we'll assume the standard mispar as the "gold standard" for our exploration of Jewish Mysticism.

Gematria is not limited to the mystics, though. It has also been used, periodically, by Rabbis in traditional Judaism. But the preference is to rely on enlightened reason in the mainstream, Rabbinic Judaism.

Gematria in Literature

Central to Jewish Mysticism, gematria first appeared in Plato's works. We find its locus classicus (original example) in Jewish literature in the Baraita, written by Rabbi Eliezer in 200 CE. No longer extant, this book appears only in the form of references. Explaining the 32 rules for the study of the Hebrew Scriptures, rule number 29 is gematria.

But it's in Sefer Yetzirah that the systematic application of gematria is fully explained, as part of its treatise on the centrality of the Hebrew language to the work of Creation.

The German Jewish pietists of the 13th Century were a group of ascetic mystics that also employed gematria in the written works they produced. These were heavily influenced by Abraham Abulafia. In the mid-16th Century, Moses Cordovero wrote the Pardes Rimonim (Garden of Pomegranates) – which discussed gematria at length.

In the 17th Century, there arose a heretical sect called the Sabbateans, who also used gematria as did the 18th Century Hassidim, building on the traditions of Kabbalah.

Today, gematria continues to be used among the Hassidim.

In our next and final chapter on Kabbalah, we'll look at the Zohar – the Book of Splendor or Radiance.

Chapter Seven: The Zohar

Traditionally attributed to Shimon bar Yochai, the Zohar consists of 23 books, totaling over 1,000 pages and offering extensive commentary about the Hebrew Scriptures and spirituality. This commentary is presented as conversations held between a variety of spiritual leaders.

While tradition has the Zohar being transmitted to Moses at Sinai, then orally transmitted, it was originally composed in Aramaic, and the historical backdrop of the book illuminates the spirit in which it was written. Under the Roman occupation of Israel (63 BCE - 135 CE), Jews lived in the shadow of oppression. The Zohar's emphasis on secret knowledge, which is intended to be closely guarded, reflects the status of the Jewish people in that context. The occupying forces were focused on limiting the influence of contemporary Rabbis, and so, many were martyred, including the mentor of bar Yochai, Rabbi Akiva.

Shortly after Rabbi Akiva's martyrdom, bar Yochai received a message he was in danger of meeting a similar fate, so he fled with his son, living in a cave for 13 years. During this time, Shimon bar Yochai (known as Rashbi) is said to have produced the Zohar.

Not widely known until the 13th Century, the Zohar was studiously guarded until Moses de Leon finally published it in Spain. There is a great deal of debate about the authorship of the Zohar, and many say that de Leon is the actual author of the book, writing in Aramaic to lend the appearance of antiquity.

Understanding the texts of the Zohar is a challenge, even for those initiated into the study of Kabbalah. Purported to contain "locks" to limit promiscuous transmission, it both reveals and conceals. Only in 2018 was an English translation published. Thus, the language barrier limited those who might read it to people able to read either the original Aramaic or the Medieval Hebrew.

The Zohar's largest themes concern the cosmos, the Divine's nature, and how the world was created. Also discussed is God's relationship to Creation via the sefirot, how the Torah was revealed, sin and evil, the ten Commandments, prayer, ancient Temple practices, the priest's role, and Exilic experiences, and Holidays.

Following the order of the books of the Torah, the Zohar contains multiple sermons, but these take on a highly mystical aspect, as they describe characters in the Bible as "soul states" and as bearers of the Divine. The book takes the form of narrative and journey, in which a group of Jewish mystics travels through the Holy Land with Rashbi, himself, discussing the Torah. The narrative represents the spiritually hungry soul's journey toward understanding the Torah on a deeper, more personal level.

The Tree of Life and the sefirot also figure prominently in the Zohar and are presented not only as emanations of Divine nature but as a "road map" to individual spiritual experience. The goal of enlightenment is served by study for the work's author. So, the study is presented as the most potent form of spirituality and the pinnacle of religious practice.

Spiritual Eroticism

Kabbalah seeks to unite God with humanity, using the vehicle of contemplation. Spiritual contemplation in the context of Zohar is an erotically charged process. Building the relationship over a candle burning in the deepest night, seeking God in Kabbalah is seeking the presence of a lover. With God depicted as the bride (Shekinah, the Divine Presence), the student seeks union, and because Divine Presence becomes lost to the world. This is known in Hebrew as devekut or Divine attachment. Sexually charged imagery is common in the Zohar, and birthing imagery, describing the physical manifestations of the love at the heart of Creation.

Central to Zoharic erotic imagery is the opening sequence of the Song of Songs (also called the Song of Solomon or the Canticle of Canticles), which reads, "Oh that he would kiss me with the kisses of his mouth" (Song of Songs 1:2).

The Song of Songs is unique in the canon of Hebrew Scripture, appearing in the Ketuvim (writings). There is no religious instruction in the book. There is no discussion of the Law or of God. Then again – Judaism considers the book to be a description of the relationship of God with humanity.

Filled with sexual imagery of the desire between two lovers, this book of the Bible is closely aligned with Zohar's sexual imagery. Commentaries on the Song of Songs follow Neoplatonic explanations of eros or erotic love, including minutely detailed expository descriptions of the act of kissing. Descriptions like these may also be found in Arabic Muslim literature like the Epistle on the Essence of Love.

Kissing is described uniformly in this and other texts from the Arab World as the joining of the breaths of people kissing (which follows the animation of the mud doll in the Genesis Creative narrative by way of the Divine breath or ruach). The joining of hearts then follows this joining of the breaths.

Moses ibn Tibbon (13th Century, Marseilles, France) was heavily influenced by the producers of these texts, the Brethren of Purity, as that influence is found in abundance in his commentary on the Song of Songs. Tibbon reads the act of kissing allegorically, reflecting Neoplatonism's idea that the soul is fascinated with intellect's beauty.

In Zohar, the kiss is seen as in the realm of the sefirot, with the entities kissing and permeating one another. The active agent of the soul in this scenario is the intellect. Fascinated with the intellect's beauty, the soul surrenders to the kiss, achieving union with the Divine.

The kiss expresses the love between the Divine and Creation, joining them in eternal union and one love not just shared but which mutually permeates them. They become enmeshed, their essences merging and becoming consubstantial. As in intense human love, it's difficult to discern where one begins and the other ends.

In Neoplatonism, the soul proceeds from the intellect and, in recognizing it, returns to its home. The influence of this Hellenistic system of philosophy can't be denied in the Zohar, as the same sequence of events and spiritual eroticism exists in its pages.

Zohar and the Spanish Expulsion

The Expulsion of the Jews from Spain in 1492 is another pivotal moment in Kabbalah's development. Before that event, though, Spain's mystics rose to the fore of Kabbalistic development. As with the destruction of the First and Second Temples, the Jewish people turned toward contemplating eschatology (the end of all things) and the appearance of the Messiah.

In Spain, the 13th Century can be characterized as a Golden Age of Kabbalah. We find Abraham Abulafia here and many others whose work has been lost to time. But this is the time of Moses de Leon's production of the Zohar (whether from bar Yochai's original or from orally transmitted knowledge emanating from antiquity).

Having been heavily influenced by Ashkenazi Hassidism, Abraham Abulafia advanced a Kabbalistic thought framework that looks familiar to us today. Rooted in ecstasy and contemplative prayer, Abulafia believed that committed adherence to Kabbalah and its doctrines had the potential to elevate the practitioner to the prophetic level.

His fascination with the aleph bet's possibilities to reveal what was concealed was focused on Torah. Moshe Idel, a noted scholar of Kabbalah, some of whose work is cited in this book, explains that Abulafia saw the Torah as the premier text of Judaism. In Torah, Abulafia saw the fullness of the intellect and the even as a Divine's mirror image.

Added to this viewpoint was his conceptualization of the Torah as describing mystics' psychological constitution and processes. This diverged from contemporaries who saw the Torah in symbolic terms, describing the life of the sefirot.

Abulafia also asserted that he was a disciple of Maimonides, known for this extreme rationalism. This is interesting, as while Kabbalah is deeply intellectual, it transcends rationalism. But Abulafia believed that his work was an expansion of that done by Maimonides in the Guide for the Perplexed, which forwarded an Aristotelian framework for understanding the Divine and Creation, as expressed in the Greek philosopher's exposition of forms (primordially existing prototypes). So perhaps it might be said that Maimonides was transformed through the lens of mysticism to arrive at a conclusion he might never have imagined.

But it was Abraham Abulafia's influence on Moses de Leon, which was to transform Kabbalistic thought, and the traditional thinking of Rabbinical Judaism, through the Zohar. But this wasn't recognized until the 20th Century.

The dark side to the flowering of Judaism in Spain and Kabbalah is the repression faced by Jews in the Iberian Peninsula of the 13th Century. But it is precisely in times of extreme pressure on the Jewish people that some of its most towering achievements have arisen.

Centered in northern Spain, in the provinces of Castilia and Catalonia, the traditions the Spanish Kabbalists drew on emanated from Provence, in France, and from Germany. And while Gershom Scholem points out that Christian influence on these writings can be proven, it's clear that the Jewish Diaspora and the tradition of oral transmission had much more to do with developing Jewish culture and tradition in Spain before 1492.

Moses de Leon

The Zohar's link to traditional Judaism is further crystallized in Moses de Leon. Like Abraham Abulafia, he was intensely engaged with the writing and thought of Maimonides.

But at some point, in the late 1250s or early 1260s, Moses de Leon turned away from rationalism and toward Kabbalah. To further immerse himself, he circulated in Castilia, engaging with the Jewish mystical community there.

In the spiritually and intellectually rich context of Castilia, de Leon entered a period of intense study, which he undertook to respond to the insurgence of rationalism (even though once a proponent of rationalism's rabbinical poster child, Maimonides).

Near the end of the 1270s, he committed his thoughts to writing, crediting antiquity sages as being responsible for it. He formulated these writings to disseminate Kabbalah by way of sharing his unique vision of it.

From this period, his writings form the Midrash ha Ne' elam (The Mystical Midrash), which later served as the Zohar's centerpiece and would come to assert tremendous influence in the Jewish World. The Zohar is the most influential example of Jewish literature to emerge after the Talmudic period.

The Zohar's Influence

The earliest publication of the Zohar was to take place between 1558 and 1560 in Mantua and Cremona, Italy. These events led to tremendous controversy among Kabbalah's followers.

The debate arising pitted purists who believe that publication was forbidden, as putting the knowledge in the hands of the uninitiated was undesirable, against those who considered such dissemination necessary for the sake of healing Creation.

Following the Expulsion, the Zohar was to become a highly regarded text, even expounded upon by traditionalists, with some of its doctrines entering the traditionalist canon of law. But wherever the Zohar went, the controversy would follow, as purists viewed its contents as a threat to the integrity of tradition.

And while controversy remains to this day, Zohar is considered an intrinsic part of the Jewish canon of religious literature, elevated to the status of the Hebrew Scripture and Talmud by the Hassidim. The founder of Hassidism, Baal Shem Tov (1698 - 1760), carried the Zohar on his person, relating that he saw Creation's fullness in its teachings. And the Vilna Gaon (1720 - 1797), while fiercely opposed to Hassidism, acknowledged the status of Zohar as a Holy book. This was the overall position of the Mitnagdim (objectors to Hassidism), who also accepted the sanctity of Zohar.

Today, the influence of the Zohar continues unabated, even though branches of Judaism (Conservative and Reform) continue to wrestle with its prominence and position in Jewish religious literature. They recognize the beauty, significance, and intellectual content of the Zohar.

This almost completes our discussion of Kabbalah but before we move on to the final portion of this book, let's make a brief stop in the world of popular Kabbalah in its modern setting, where we'll find proponents like pop Diva Madonna.

Chapter Eight: Kabbalah Gone Wild

The esoteric has long been a fascination for people in high places. During the Victorian Era, for example, high society loved to dabble in the occult, conjuring the spirits at tony seances and consulting Ouija boards to check in on departed love ones.

But the enthusiasm for Kabbalah in the dabbler's, celebrity, and the working world is almost an ecstasy all on its own. The story goes back to 1971 and the establishment of the now internationally diffused Kabbalah Center.

The Rav

Philip Berg and his wife, Karen, were virtually penniless when they set out to create a resource for women and non-Jews to experience a simplified form of Kabbalah by opening the first Kabbalah Center in 1971 in New York City. At its pinnacle, this international learning institution boasted 40 plants located all over the world. While both taught and wrote books about their version of Kabbalah, Berg came to be known as "the Rav." Confined to a wheelchair following a stroke, Karen and the couple's sons took the reins. The Rav died in 2013.

Associated with the Kabbalah Center is the red string bracelet, worn to protect against ayin ha ra (the evil eye). When Madonna wore the bracelet and be a regular guest at the Bergs' Shabbat table, the movement grew exponentially.

In 2006, the celebrity singer collaborated with the Bergs on her charity, Raising Malawi, a relief agency supporting the eponymous nation.

And as Madonna's devotion grew, so did the Kabbalah Center's celebrity following. Madonna included the red string bracelet on her merchandise tables at concerts, incorporating items like tefillim into her music videos. She also provided continual financial support to the Kabbalah Center. Madonna was followed into the KC by luminaries like Roseanne Barr, Sandra Bernhard, Mick Jagger, Jerry Hall, Britney Spears, Naomi Campbell, fashion designer Donna Karan, Elizabeth Taylor, and Lindsay Lohan.

The Trouble with Pop Spirituality

The version of Kabbalah circulated by the Kabbalah Center varies wildly from the original impetus of the canon itself and its interpretation through time. Rather than the noble project of repairing the relationship between the Creator and the Created Order, KC promises the realization of personal dreams. This focus closely follows that of other popularized religious institutions, including the Christian churches that forward the "prosperity theology," which promises wealth to followers who obey the church's confessional formula in a question.

But Judaism has a similar strand of personalized Faith in the Lubavitchers, especially about their evangelical efforts in the nation of Israel. Evangelizing is forbidden in Judaism, with those interested in joining the Faith being refused three times by a Rabbi before they can begin the process of doing so. However, the "Lubavitchers" are known to distribute items like boxes containing vials of "holy water," blessed by the (long dead) Rabbi Menachim Mendel Schneerson. This project is aimed at Jews who are "in name only" or of branches of Judaism, which are less prescriptive, especially in terms of the order of daily life.

I would not have believed it had I not seen one such box with my own eyes. But my eyes were treated to the image of Rabbi Schneerson smiling out from every blank wall, telephone box, every possible surface to which a poster might be affixed, throughout the Holy Land, during my visit in 2006.

Since the Rebbe's death in 1994, his disciples have enthusiastically distributed the mayim chaim (living water), claiming that just one drop of the miraculous water can transform regular water into mayim chaim. And why? Because the "Lubavitcher Rebbe" was the long-awaited Messiah, in their opinion.

A 1996 article in the Jewish News of Northern California details some claims of his disciples in Jerusalem, where the water is distributed from Beit Mosheach (House of the Messiah). Miraculous cures are claimed, just as Madonna once asserted that a similar "miraculous" water offered by the Kabbalah Center would solve the "nuclear problems of the world."

And lest you believe that late-stage capitalism was not the driving force behind the Lubavitcher mayim chaim, you should know that in 1996, Beit Mosheach was not selling the water but suggesting a rather sizeable donation of 28 x 28 shekels ($260). Not exactly bus fare for a small vial of water.

While Chabad Lubavitch characterizes the mayim chaim as the work of a fringe tendency under the umbrella of the Lubavitchers and the practice of distributing has been condemned by the Chabad Court, it was 10 years after this article was published that I saw that odd artifact in Tel Aviv, Israel.

The problem with pop spirituality is that it's a form of populism that takes the same shape as the political version. It flattens the intellectual component of the practices and knowledge associated with discipleship, producing a bland round of pita that sustains only the individual and their ambitions. It promises miracles without demanding introspection. In both these cases of the misappropriation of spirituality in pursuing producing disciples (and money), we see Kabbalah reduced to a plastic bead's status when it is a diamond.

Questionable Practices

Upon learning that God had 72 names, Britney Spears had one tattooed on her neck. She did this because of the Kabbalah's Center's claim that all your dreams will come true if you meditate on these names.

This narcissistic image of spirituality deviates from the gravity of Kabbalah as a humble system of intellectually informed practice that leads the follower into union with God. And that is not a selfish pursuit. Rather, that union is pursued in the universal project of Kabbalah - tikkun - the total restoration of the Created Order to make way for the promised Messiah (who is not the Lubavitcher Rebbe, by most accounts).

The Kabbalah Center also claims that it's not even necessary for followers to read or understand the Zohar. Merely having it with you is enough to protect yourself from evil. This belief reduces one of the most important works of Jewish religious literature to an evil eye pendant's status.

Karen Berg has even stated that the Zohar is a "bar code" from which meaning, and power may be derived without understanding the text's words. Merely by scanning the Zohar, she insists, you may partake of its Divine message. Pity the poor apocryphal author, hiding in a cave from the Roman occupiers and scribbling in its darkness in desolation. The arrogance of such claims is almost unbearable.

And as the Bergs were to discover, all the red string and "miraculous" water in the world can't save you from the wrath of a God who will not be mocked.

The Decline of the Kabbalah Center

The Rav died in 2013. Notably absent from his levaya (funeral) was his most famous student, Madonna. In 2011, the singer disassociated herself from the Kabbalah Center, cutting all ties between it and her Raising Malawi charity.

At issue was almost $4 million dollars spent on building what was to be a school for girls, which was never built. Following an audit, Madonna removed the Board of Directors, replacing it with a provisional Board. The audit revealed outrageous expenditures for items like salaries, golf course fees, and a car and driver for the Board's Chair.

Following the audit, the CIA and FBI investigated Raising Malawi for "financial malfeasance" associated with the misappropriated funds. In 2013, the charity was sued by two donors, claiming misuse of $1 million of their funding and seeking $40 million in damages. The plaintiffs claimed that the Center pressured students to "give until it hurt" if they wanted to receive "the light" (of Kabbalah) And in 2015, one of the Bergs' sons, Yehuda, was accused of causing emotional distress to a student and the Kabbalah Center was instructed to pay damages of $42,500. Yehuda Berg was ordered to pay restitution of $135,000. Sexual battery and the provision of drugs and alcohol were both alleged. Yehuda was to subsequently reveal that he was addicted to drugs and alcohol.

Just last year, Yehuda Berg was interviewed by Vice News, expressing his interest in again establishing himself as a spiritual authority, even in the face of all that had transpired. But his latest means of spiritual support, he hopes, will be as an addictions and crisis management counselor.

The Kabbalah Center, now divested of Yehuda, continues to operate, overseeing 40 locations in North and South America, Europe, Oceania/Asia, the Middle East, and Africa.

Instructive as this tale is, perhaps it's appropriately illuminated by this saying from Talmud, which instructs, "When a camel tries to get horns, his ears are cut off" (Sanhedrin 106a).

Chapter Nine: The Ashkenazi Hassidim – In the Ashes of the Crusades

Before we delve into the subject of the Ashkenazi Hassidim, it's important to note this is not an ideologically consistent group. Rather, there are numerous sects of devotion throughout the greater movement, organized around rabbinical personalities, something we'll read about in this chapter.

The Lubavitcher sect's example from the last chapter is just one example of the diversity inherent in this larger group. Today, when we hear of intractable communities like those in New York City, which refuse to wear masks and continue to hold large gatherings in defiance of city and state prohibitions, it must be remembered that these actions are not representative of the whole. However, they do point to history and the response of Jewish communities to the threats presented to it.

Ashkenazi Hassidism has a long and storied history, and one of the most central themes in that history is this branch of Judaism's embrace of the Kabbalah. Intensely mystical, while also intensely legalistic, the Hassidim bring us some of the most colorful and fascinating tales, only a fraction of which are related in Tales of the Hassidim by Martin Buber.

First, let's explore the history and development of Ashkenazi Hassidism. From there, we'll move on to some related and perhaps, illuminating contemporary information.

Medieval Hassidism

While Ashkenazi Hassidism (German Pietism) arose out of Germany, its roots were exported from Italy. The Kalonymos family left Italy for Germany, arriving in the 9th Century and flourishing until the 13th Century, in locations along the Rhine River.

If that name sounds Greek to you, you're right. The Kalonymos name can be found in Greece, Italy, and Provence, France. In Ancient Greek, it means "good name," which is a direct translation of the Hebrew "Shem Tov" (shem - name, tov - good). Later in this section, you'll see how "Shem Tov" will figure prominently in the development of Ashkenazi Hassidism.

A family emigrating to another country may not sound like a big deal to you, but the Kalonymos family was to become the foundation of what we recognize as Askenazi Hassidism.

While the roots of the family can be traced to 8th Century Italy, the name also occurs in Talmudic literature (Avodah Zarah 11a). But the name was very common in Medieval times and doesn't always indicate a familial connection to this foundational family, which is the locus classicus of Hassidism.

The Kolonymos family was imminently learned, having in its rank's rabbis, theologians, and authors. The influence they exerted was, therefore, considerable. This family was to lead Jewish communities in the Rhineland throughout the terrors of the Crusades. This was especially so during the First Crusade's intense persecution of the Jews and the chaos of the 12th and 13th Centuries, as the Christians continued their Crusade to control the Holy Land.

During the later centuries, Ashkenazi Hassidism was born, combining extreme austerity with mysticism. The movement aimed to bring marginal practitioners into a more spiritual and religious lifestyle. Due to the Crusades and all the horror, these entailed for Jews, Hassidism arose as a religious/spiritual response that guided, transcend, and heal souls experiencing the manifestation of brutal anti-Semitism.

During the first period, three leaders emerged from the Kalonymos family, namely: Samuel ben Kalonymos, Judah ben Samuel (the Chasid of Regensberg and son of Samuel ben Kalonymos), and Eleazar ben Judah of Worms.

All three had brought with them the mystical traditions of Kabbalah as they existed in that time, including intense knowledge of Merkavah Mysticism. But their approach was rooted in the love of God and humility. In this early layer of Ashkenazi Hassidism, offering penitence was central to its practice, giving the movement an air of extreme asceticism not seen in later Hassidism.

Sefer Hassidim

The Book of the Pious (Sefer Hassidim) is the foundation of Ashkenazi Hassidim ("The Pious of Germany"). It details the daily devotional life of Jews in Germany during the Middle Ages. Authored by Judah ben Samuel of Regensburg, it compiles the teaching of the three central leaders of the movement during the 12th and 13th Centuries (those named in the last section).

Teachings laid out in Sefer Hassidim focus on ascetic, mystical, and ethical teachings, touching on the practice of piety, repentance, the afterlife, reward, and punishment. Arranged into a variety of headings, it also details fasting and feast days, sin, martyrdom, and Torah's study.

The book first appeared in Hebrew in the late 12th and early 13th Centuries in the Rhineland, soon after the Second Crusade. Following its introduction, it was diffused widely, having a heavy influence on the German Hassidic community's highly distinctive practices, which spoke and continues to speak a version of "High" German called Yiddish. The Book of the Pious has also helped to establish a framework for Jewish ethics far beyond its original regional and historical setting. Since 1538, it has been reprinted in multiple editions in a variety of formats, accompanied by numerous detailed commentaries.

The Hassidim's primary influence in this time was the Sefer Yetzirah, accompanied by the Sefer ha-Bahir. Those mystical traditions found their way into Hassidic practice via the teachings in the Sefer Hassidim.

But what events gave birth to Ashkenazi Hassidism? Undoubtedly, the brutality of the Crusades was fundamental to provoking the establishment of this form of Jewish Pietism. Just as the Jews had turned inward in the wake of the destruction of the Temples, this latter group was to similarly seek God's presence as a salve for the disastrous impact of the Crusades on Jewish communities in Europe (the Rhineland, especially) and in the Holy Land. Understanding the impact of the Crusades is thus foundational to understanding where Ashkenazi Hassidism came from.

The First Crusade

On November 27, 1095, Pope Urban II preached at Clermont-Ferrand, declaring that God had commanded a Holy War against the Muslim Faith to restore the Holy Land to Christian control. Declaring "Deus vult!" ("God wills it!"), there was no implicit threat in the speech, one of the most pivotal of the Middle Ages. But Jews in France weren't convinced and set out to warn the Rhineland communities of impending danger.

The pilgrimage route to the Holy Land traditionally followed the Rhine and Danube rivers in these times, and the wealthy communities of the Rhine were directly in the line of fire. With Crusaders mustering along the pilgrimage route, Godfrey of Bouillon (1060 – 1100) vowed to avenge the Crucifixion by murdering as many Jews as possible.

Peter the Hermit (circa 1050 – unknown) was a key figure in the First Crusade. A revivalist and fiery, populist preacher, he was instrumental in both recruiting Christian peasants to the cause and drawing the Faithful from France, Holland, and England.

When the Crusaders arrived in Cologne, the Jews were not disturbed. This may have been by the grace of a letter delivered to Peter the Hermit, offering to supply his Crusaders with provisions in return for leaving Jewish communities in peace.

This peace lasted for no more than a month. The Crusaders' fervor gained momentum as more and more of them arrived, feeding off one another's communal outrage and building to a frenzy of religiously motivated bloodlust. Jewish communities in the region knew that Peter's promise was unlikely to hold in the face of such a rabble.

Leaders of the Mainz community then sent a delegation to the Holy Roman Emperor of the day, Henry IV, who immediately wrote to leaders in the ranks of the Crusaders to leave the Jews in peace. As insurance, the Mainz and Cologne communities offered a tribute to the Emperor. While the leaders of the Crusades were inclined to follow the Emperor, the common people who'd been stirred to join them were not so amenable. Highly susceptible to anti-Semitic propaganda being disseminated in the ranks of the gathering Crusaders.

The problem was that the Crusaders' noble elements believed dissent to be undesirable, considering the nature of the Crusades. They didn't want to see Christians pitted against Christian over the treatment of the Jews. And so, between the Holidays of Pesach and

Shavuot, the violence started and continued, unabated, until the summer of that year.

On May 03, 1096, the synagogue at Speyer was surrounded by the Crusaders. Finding it impossible to break-in, the assembled rabble attacked any Jews found in its vicinity, and eleven were killed. One of them was a woman who refused to convert to Christianity, choosing martyrdom. This was the choice provided by the Crusaders – conversion or death. In response, the tradition of Kiddush ha-Shem (Martyrdom for the name of God) was resurrected. This tradition had begun in antiquity at the fortress Masada in the Holy Land in 100 CE, during which Jewish Sicarii (assassins) and residents there committed suicide in the face of Roman victory.

Later, In May 1096, the city of Worms was similarly attacked, first with Jews killed in their homes and then, in the bishop's palace, where they'd sought refuge but had been betrayed. Approximately 800 Jews died during this siege, having chosen Kiddush ha-Shem over the conversion to Christianity.

From there, the massacres continued, arriving at Mainz and Cologne, continuing through Bohemia. Approximately 5,000 Jewish deaths are recorded. The scenario is reminiscent of the modern genocide in Rwanda. Overtaken by messages of hatred pouring from the radio, 800,000 people were murdered (mostly with machetes) in only 100 days. The bloodlust incited by the power of words had resulted in communal insanity. This very insanity led the Hungarians to stop the Crusaders, rising against their unhinged, genocidal spree.

With the Crusaders routed, the Rhineland Jews and those in other communities along the pilgrimage route were left to sift through their communities' rubble and shattered lives.

Reaching the Holy Land in June of 1099, the Crusaders captured Jerusalem the following month, and Godfrey of Bouillon entered through the Jewish Quarter. Joining forces with the Muslims, the Jews fought back and eventually were driven into synagogues, which were burned. All survivors were sold into slavery. Some of these were later to emerge as free people due to the efforts of Italian Jews.

While the community in Jerusalem was wiped out and could not return, Galilee was untouched. But both Ramleh and Jaffa were dispersed, leaving the Jewish presence in the Holy Land a mere shadow.

Second Crusade

Aggression against Jewish communities was to continue in various forms in the period between the First and Second Crusades, with the Popes of the day fervently preaching for a new crusade. In 1198, Innocent III forbade interest on Crusader debt and demanded that any monies already paid should be returned to them, exacting a heavy financial toll on Jewish lenders.

During this period, the Popes of the Roman Empire had a propensity for attaching the word "Crusade" to any interest they had, thus sanctifying it. With Jewish financial interests under siege, it was not long before the violence began anew.

In the summer 0f 1146, renewed attacks on the Rhineland communities commenced. These were inflamed by the preaching of the monk, Radulph, who exhorted the Crusaders to avenge the Crucifixion by attacking Jews on their way to the Holy Land to attack the Muslims.

The attacks prompted Bernard of Clairveaux (1090 – 1153) to point out the theological error in Rudolph's assignment of blame to the Jews. And while rioting in Jewish communities by Crusaders was already in progress, his intervention was responsible for greatly limiting carnage on the scale of the First Crusade, despite random incidences, primarily in the Rhineland.

Across Europe, Jews could denounce their false conversions to Christianity and return to their native religion. By 1147, peace and order had been restored, with communities re-establishing along the Rhine.

In the Holy Land, Jews had re-established themselves outside Jerusalem, while few remained in the Holy City. During the Second Crusade, the rash of violence experienced in the First was greatly reduced.

In 1187, the Crusaders fell to Saladin, and again, the Jews of Europe were anticipated to pay the price. But in 1182, Emperor Frederick I pledged his protection, at great cost to the Jews of the Rhineland in the payment of tribute. Penalties were issued again, implicated Crusaders, following continuing threats to Jewish communities in 1188. But Imperial protective orders left Jews at the mercy of the Roman Empire and its shifting whims, creating extreme uncertainty.

Third Crusade

Taking place from 1189 through 1192, the Third Crusade arose in England, France, and in the Holy Roman Empire to reclaim the Holy Land from Saladin. Richard the Lionheart (Richard I, 1157-1199), newly crowned, proclaimed his intention to participate. Across England, Jewish communities were massacred wholesale.

In York, the local nobility saw in the Crusade a chance to divest themselves of debt, slaughtering any Jews who remained in the town, after many had sought refuge in the Castle Keep.

On March 06 of that year, Rabbi Isaac of Joigny saw that the Crusades were again about to destroy the Jewish people, telling the community that Kaddush ha-Shem was preferable to forced conversion. 150 members of the community set their possessions on fire and killed themselves. Those who didn't were killed by the

Crusader mob. The ledger of debts was destroyed, thus achieving the cynical ambitions of the indebted nobility.

With King Richard off crusading, there was little to stop the genocidal madness, but it was not as though Richard was an inclined act. The Jewish community of Europe had lost faith in the West and its violent adventures, and in 1211, 300 rabbis left Western Europe for the Holy Land.

And they were not wrong to do so, for into the 1300s, crusading continued. While most of Europe was peaceful, in France, the Pastoureaux (the "Shepherds) was to continue the bloody tradition in 1320. A veritable rabble of 40,000, with an average age of 16, marched throughout the country, killing Jews wantonly. While Pope John XXII excommunicated all who could be identified with this de facto (unauthorized and unorganized) Crusade, this action did little to tame their ardor. Along the River Loire alone, these hooligans destroyed 120 Jewish communities.

When the Pastoureaux crossed the Pyrenees into Spain, James II of Aragon forced the dispersal of the mob. But the damage to Jewish communities in France and Spain had been cataclysmic.

Aftermath

Despite issuing the Sicut Judaeis (Papal Bull entitled "As the Jews") by Pope Callixtus II (1119 - 1124), which commanded protection of the Jews and was issued multiple times between 1199 and 1250, the anti-Semitism of the Church remained intact in its doctrines and preaching.

The historical animus of the Church against the Jews existed in Europe well before the Crusades and, despite the efforts of leadership to contain it, repeatedly erupted in violence and forced conversion, forbidden by Sicut Judaeis.

Even though the record of the Christian Scriptures and history itself demonstrates that the Jews were under the control of the Roman Empire at the time of the Crucifixion and thus, as subject to violence themselves as any other occupied entity, the claim of Jewish hostility against Christianity was pervasive. This led to the claims of Blood Libel.

Beginning the 12th Century, Blood Libel claimed a conspiracy by Jews to sacrifice Christians – one each year - with the victims being selected at an annual meeting. This led to the Blois massacre in 1171, where every Jew who lived there was burned at stake in retribution for this hate-fueled conspiracy theory. In Germany, Blood Libel claims circulated in the 13th Century.

The Crusades, continuing through 1270, were eight in total and while the object was said to be the establishment of Christian rule in Jerusalem, the toll exacted on the Jews of Europe and in the Holy Land tells a tale of ancient animosity. At the heart of that animosity was the resentment against Jews generated by their refusal to acknowledge Jesus as the promised Messiah. In maintaining their religious identity unto death, and stubbornly refusing to convert to Christianity, the animus against the Jews was only to grow over the centuries, punctuated by periods of relative safety and peace.

In this crucible was born the spiritual movement of the Ashkenazi Hassidim, answering the evil of the world around it with dedicated, quasi-separatist pietism.

Chapter Ten: Rising Up in Piety - Baal Shem Tov and the Hassidic Renaissance

Our story of the birth of modern Hassidism begins with Israel ben Eliezer, later to be called the Baal Shem Tov (circa 1698 - 1760), which is abbreviated to the acronym "Besht" and means "Master of the Good Name."

Considered the founder of Hassidism, the Baal Shem Tov changed the face of Judaism, reviving it after centuries of oppression. His impact has been felt throughout the Jewish World.

After the Rhineland suffered under the Crusaders, Eastern European Judaism suffered under the pogroms, occurring in 1648 through 1649. These took the lives of 10s of thousands of Jews.

The pogroms also deprived Jews of the ability to make a decent living, plunging the survivors into abject poverty. That estate prevented thousands of young people from pursuing a traditional education in the study of Torah Talmud, giving rise to a devout but largely uneducated Jewish underclass. It was into this underclass that the Baal Shem Tov was born in the town of Okop, then on the Polish/Russian frontier.

Because of the Baal Shem Tov's humble origins and his importance to modern Judaism, there are many conflicting stories about his early life, but a common detail in them all is the loss of his parents in childhood.

After the death of his parents, young Yisrael would be cared for by the community, and while it's not known precisely what sort of education he received in that context, it can be safely assumed that he had the same level of access to education as other children of his humble class.

But this little boy was quite different from the others. When not studying, he could be found wandering in nature. He was known, in his youth, to have a vibrant relationship with God. From this root grew his later teachings and philosophies, which helped to establish the pietist Hassidic movement.

As Yisrael grew into his teens (the young adulthood of the time), the community was released from its responsibility for him, and he began to work. One of his first jobs was that of caretaker of a synagogue, opening the door to the study of Jewish literature, which he devoured. But he pursued this secretly, maintaining an air of humility. During this time, he was exposed to the canon of Kabbalah.

Again, the particulars of the Baal Shem Tov's life are shrouded in mystery, only illuminated by popular folklore. He is said to have married and then losing his wife, married again shortly thereafter. He was then was supported by his wife as he dedicated himself to study and the worship of God.

In 1734, at 36, Yisrael settled in the town of Tluste, Poland, and revealed his knowledge to the world around, something he'd hidden. Rapidly, he came to be known as a sage and subsequently, as the Baal Shem Tov.

Moving to Medzeboz in Western Ukraine, he was to settle and remain there for the rest of his life. Here, he taught and preached, basing most of his teachings on those of Isaac Luria. The Baal Shem

Tov did something differently, though, to simplify those teachings, making them accessible to Jews who hadn't been granted the virtue of education. He further emphasized the centrally of mentorship and being in a close relationship with one who had command of the Torah. Further, he taught that, while important, Torah study wasn't the only means to be in a relationship with God. For him, the mediating presence of a scholar was how Jewish young people, having lived in educational deprivation following the pogroms, could attain the full benefits of the study.

This rejection of educational elitism propelled the growth of the Hassidic movement in Eastern Europe and beyond. At the time of the Baal Shem Tov's death, the number of Hassidic followers was approximately 10,000. But thereafter, his influence and that of Hassidism continued to grow exponentially.

We only know of the Baal Shem Tov's teachings due to the diligence of his students in recording them, especially Rabbi Yacob Yosef of Polonoye (1710 – 1784). Authoring several books, he is largely responsible for disseminating hundreds of Baal Shem Tov quotations in his writing.

At the heart of the Baal Shem Tov's teachings is the love of the nation of Israel and its people, and this heart is also that of the movement he founded - Ashkenazi Hassidim, a religious impulse which places love, humility, piety, and joy above all worldly considerations.

Napoleon's Russian Campaign (1769-1821)

As you've just read in the story of the Baal Shem Tov, Polish Jews in the times that he was born had been stripped of any vestige of prosperity by the pogroms they'd suffered. But in the first half of the 18th Century, Poland was partitioned, dividing communities in the country. This exposed Polish Jewry to a variety of influences, including Russian, Austro-Hungarian, and Prussian.

Hassidism had already been diffused through Ukraine, central Poland, Galacia, Lithuania, Belarus, and Hungary. Because of the diverse cultural contexts into which Hassidism was interpolated, Hassidism is extremely diverse in its expressions, wherever it's found.

But formative in developing the movement is Napolean's Russian Campaign. Viewed by some in the movement as the Armageddon of the day, or the war of "Gog and Magog," they saw Napolean's push into Russia as the preamble to the Messiah's coming.

The political intricacies of the region led to some Hassidim supporting Napoleon and others rejecting him. This led to the degradation of rabbinical authority – a pillar of Jewish tradition. A void formed in the traditional order, into which the Hassidim rushed.

And they were ready, having established a parallel structure to traditional Judaism, which focused on the relationship between Rabbis and their successors. This is the beginning of the Hassidic dynasties, rooted in the personal charisma of individual "tzadikkim" (righteous ones).

Hassidic Dynasties

The disciple of the Baal Shem Tov, Yacov Yosef of Polonoye, and later, Elimelech of Lizhensk (1717 – 1787) created the doctrine of the "Tzadik," forming a theological basis for the structure, which extended into the social order of Jewish communities. And just as the Baal Shem Tov had insisted that even those individuals who had not attained mastery of the Torah could ascend to a personal relationship with God, tzadikkism invested the Rabbi with authority. While Baal Shem Tov's model of mentorship was a personal one between the teacher and his student, tzadikkism extended that relationship to the entire community of which the teacher was the resident Tzadik.

In this model, divine grace was extended to the community through the righteousness of the Tzadik, creating dynastic succession through authoritative figures within Hassidism, with explicit teachings, philosophies, and community rules, varying from one community to the next. With the mass of followers described as "Hassidim," the model of the community itself gave rise to the diversity of thought.

Hassidic dynasties began to be named according to the birthplaces of their Rabbis. For example, "Vizhnitzer Hassidim" was named after the town of Vyzhnytsia in the Ukraine, where Menachim Mendel Hager (1830 - 1884) was born, and "Gerer Hassidism" after the town of Gora Kalwari, where Rabbi Yitzchak Meir Rothenburg Aler (1798 - 1866) was born.

One of the most important Hassidic dynasties was that of Rabbi Nachman of Bratslav (1771-1810). As a grandson of the Baal Shem Tov, he was deeply invested in the Hassidism of earlier times, emphasizing his grandfather's call to Holiness, one-on-one instruction, and humility. Rabbi Nachman is especially remembered for his stories, later memorialized by Martin Buber in Tales of the Hassidim. After his death, Rabbi Nachman was revered by his followers as the only Tzadik. They await his return, to this day.

And while the Bratslav Dynasty is key, there is no Hassidic Dynasty more widely known than the Lubavitchers, who we discussed briefly in the Chapter entitled "Kabbalah Gone Wild."

Named after the home of the dynasty's second Rabbi, who was not born in the town (but set down roots in 1813), the Lubavitcher dynasty takes the name of the western Russian city of Lyubavhichi. Founded by Rabbi Schneur Zalman of Liabi (1745 - 1813), this dynasty was to become one of the most influential.

Experiencing conflict with his Lithuanian neighbors, Rabbi Zalman published the Tanya, meaning "we have learned" in Aramaic. In this, he forwarded an esoteric framework combining traditional rabbinical rationalism derived from Kabbalistic influences with Hassidic Mysticism.

The Lubavitchers are called "Chabad" Hassidism, combining Jewish Mysticism with rational Judaism in a vibrant and highly defined way. The word "Chabad" is formed from an acronym for three of the sefirot from the Tree of Life, including Da'at (knowledge - which is not included in all forms of the Tree by that name). The other two sefirot, which form the root of the word, are Chockmah and Binah. So, Chabad is the union of knowledge, wisdom, and understanding.

Advancing "rational Hassidism," the Lubavitchers answered their Lithuanian opponents by (in essence) reducing the influence of the Tzadik. This was achieved by maintaining the sage's authority but removing the cult of personality associated with the Tzadikkim of Hassidic dynasties, and the Messianic aspects. Later manifestations of Hassidism have altered this feature over time, as you'll remember from our discussion of the Holy Water allegedly blessed by Rabbi Schneerson.

About the Lubavitcher Rebbe, from this branch of Hassidism, the structure of its modern evolution may be readily seen, whereby both the Messianic importance of the Rebbe and his charism has been robustly restored. This modern movement is intensely revivalist in every aspect of its community life. Furthering this theme, Chabad is dedicated to religious education for Jews, with a clear agenda of furthering its vision of community. From the perspective of Jewish Mysticism and its appeal to the healing of the relationship between God and Creation, the Lubavitchers take the mission seriously.

The Mitnagdim

Because of the Sabbatean controversy of the 17th Century, in which Sabbatei Zevi (1626 - 1676) was advanced as the Messiah out of Galilee in the Holy Land and proclaimed to be so by Nathan of Gaza (1643 - 1680) in 1666.

Fearing a repeat performance of that relatively recent heresy, traditionalists were highly suspicious of Hassidism. This was in response to subtle changes made by the movement to items like the prayer times and rearranging the words in some prayers. Of these changes, the most significant was that made to the halakha (Jewish Law), concerning a knife used for kosher butchering.

None of the changes was substantive, and the reaction from representatives of traditional Judaism may be viewed as somewhat "petty." But the changes made by the Hassidim represented enough of a deviation from accepted tradition to threaten the existing order.

What traditional Rabbinical Judaism was most concerned with was the position of the Tzadik. That this leader could perform religious obligations on behalf of his community was considered deeply threatening to the life and practice of all Jews. Strengthening this position was a perceived lack of gravity on the part of the Hassidim about ritual. Also problematic was that the Hassidim weren't afraid to use liquor to simulate the sensation of union with the Divine.

At the heart of this Hassidic innovation is the belief that God could be served by both the yetzer ha-rah and the yetzer ha-tov (the evil and the good urges). As we've learned earlier in this book, both these impulses are related to the shattering of the vessels. Good and evil are held in eternal tension, lest the world disintegrates completely. This came with the philosophy advanced by Yacov Yosef of Polonoye, stating that the Tzadik should find within himself at least a particle of evil intent to "delete" the guilt of his followers. Even via the Tzadik, the act advances the ongoing redemption of Creation and the coming of the Messiah. The implicit appeal to the grave duty of a community leader is even more philosophically harmonious and striking. Taking on the guilt of those he leads, the Tzadik takes the hit for the Hassidim in his catchment. This is an important point to remember as we move toward contemporary Hassidism.

Also, there was the matter of the habit of singing and dancing in the life of the Hassidim, raising the suspicions of the traditionalists, as this was not a feature of the contemporary Judaism of the day.

Also viewed with a jaded eye was that the charism inherent in such activities had been made possible by women, supporting the men's exertions with all the domestic work required for such an ascetic, prayer-focused existence paralleling the social organizations of their communities.

The established order believed the Hassidim to be a threat to the continuing existence of the Jews in Europe, attracting unnecessary attention and generally inviting unwelcome scrutiny from hostile communities. The Church and its rabble had not so long before Crusaded and pogromed them into poverty and communal collapse.

Organized opposition to the Hassidim first arose in Lithuania, led by Rabbi Elijah ben Schlomo Zalman (1720 – 1797), known as the Vilna Gaon. The Vilna Gaon's critique of Hassidism was focused on Mysticism and the ecstatic expressions encouraged by the movement in worship. But what he was most concerned about was the position of the Rabbi in Hassidic communities and the ignorance of the followers for whom the Tzadik acted. He believed this represented a deliberate abandonment of Torah study as a traditional feature of Jewish life, of whatever sect or movement.

This led the Vilna Gaon to become a leader of the Mitnagdim ("opponents") of the Hassidim in Lithuania. Directly confronting Chabad (Lubavitchers – yet another fascinating wrinkle) Hassidism, he moved to have the movement banned in 1772. The ban was renewed in 1781, and any literature associated with Chabad was burned. This dispute was to continue and to be exacerbated after 1790, with both the Mitnagdim and Chabad turning to secular authorities for mediation.

The conflict endured well into the 20th Century, rivaling the Hatfields and McCoys for the longevity of "grudge match." But there was an eventual cooling effect, mediated by time itself. But because the Chabad Hassidim clarified the centrality of traditional Judaism, over time, they were perceived to have restored traditionalism, centering Torah and Talmud in their proper place in the context of the movement. But the whole truth is that the true end came with the Jewish State of Czar Alexander I in December 1804. In essence, the Czar's order was that all Jews had the right to worship following their community guidelines.

But the Hassidim and the Vilna Gaon were soon to be become united Jewish Superpowers, joining forces to defeat the secularizing influence of the Haskalah.

Haskalah - The Jewish Enlightenment

The Haskalah was a social movement within Judaism during the late 18th and early 19th Centuries, with precursors in the late part of the previous century. Haskalah called for integrating the Jews into secular society. It advanced the thesis that part of this integration should be achieved through education. The Haskalah advocated for the uniqueness and integrity of the Jewish World. The movement arose as a response to changes to discriminatory legislation against Jews. These changes represented numerous opportunities for a greater societal role and a less segregated existence for Jewish people.

Called "Maskilim," the proponents of the Haskalah presented the Hassidim with a challenge to their detached, meditative, devotional structures. As for the Hassidim, the Maskilim were not about the "enlightenment" any devout Jew would take an interest in.

In Galicia (Poland), there was the deliberate effort (Galicia Maskilim) to deride and thus, discourage the practice of Hassidism. Hassidism was growing quickly in the region, with young people flocking to it. This alarmed the Maskilim, who saw Hassidism as a boulder in the road toward enlightenment.

Led by Yosef Perl (1773 - 1839), the Galicia Maskilim wrote extensively about Hassidim. They also sought the help of the State hoping to suppress the now popular movement.

Perl's contributions to the literature of the Haskalah are satirical retellings of books revered by the Hassidim, depicting adherents as mutated, deformed Jews. Perl repeatedly wrote to the government to act against the Hassidim. The assault on a visibly devoted minority in his system of Faith is shocking. Perl's devotion to the Haskalah was rooted in a desire to shuck off all the traditional trappings of his Faith and integrate. In that desire, he had inappropriately included every living Jew.

While the greater Haskalah movement can't be characterized by its Galician forebear alone, it's important to note its impact on the Hassidim of the day and the way they interpreted the aims of the Maskilim.

The Hatfields and McCoys Find Common Purpose

If you're aware that some Hassidism today revere the memory of the Vilna Gaon, you may not be quite able to understand why. Haskalah is the answer to your questions. Mutually outraged at even the vaguest suggestion they are absorbed into gentile society, the Mitnagdim and Hassidim joined forces opposing it.

Russia was to be affected by the Haskalah late in the movement. This occurred simultaneously with the impact of a second secularizing tendency, in the Science of Judaism Movement, late in the 19th Century. The Science of Judaism saw its mission as deconstructing Jewish religious literature through the lens of science.

Like their Galician forebears, the Maskilim of Russia wrote satirical pieces, following Yosef Perl, describing Hassidism in baldly unflattering terms like "fanaticism." The Science of Judaism echoed this assault, calling Hasidism having been "born in gloom."

The impact of this public narrative on the Hassidic communities of Russia was, predictably, devastating. Suddenly, the most radical tendency of Judaism had been cast as a rigidly status quo institution, dedicated to the past and not the glorious future of the Haskalah.

The Hassidic communities contracted into themselves, with the conspicuous exception of the Chabad. In these events is a temporary decline in Hassidism, which had once been a respected source of Jewish revival, intense learning, and theological evolution via the movement's Mysticism.

But in the Maskilim and Hassidim union is found the modern Haredi movement, of which Hassidim is a part. Our next chapter will explore the resurgence of Ashkenazi Hassidism in the New World.

While marginalized after about the second decade of the 19th Century, Hassidism was not to be crushed. It would become an enormous tendency and presence in modern Judaism because of a well-known and infamous historic event, which we'll discuss in our next chapter.

Chapter Eleven: The Holocaust and the Return of the Hassidim

Whether readers like it or not, no discussion may be had of any aspect of modern Judaism without entertaining the painful subject of the Holocaust. The subject is exhausting. The deeper you go within the workings of the Third Reich, the more overwhelmed and outraged by its evil you become.

As though the ancient god of the Underworld, Mot, had arisen on earth, accompanied by Baal, his priests, and had opened his jaws, Israel's people were swallowed, disappearing almost wholesale from the cities and streets of Europe.

It's not my desire to horrify the reader with the Holocaust or to make this book entirely concerned with it but its importance must be acknowledged if we are to understand the Hassidim in the wake of the Second World War and the most organized and sustained expression of hatred against Jews in history.

For the marginalized Hassidim, the Holocaust proved to be an event even more pivotal to their belief system than the destruction of the ancient Temples, the Crusades, or the pogroms. The Holocaust was the ultimate expression of hatred, an event of such searing cataclysmic proportions it rendered in its ashes an new expression of

Judaism – ultra-Orthodoxy or Haredi. This was to be the umbrella under which Hassidism fell, following the close of the Second World War.

"Why Didn't They Run Away?"

If I had a dollar for every time I'd heard someone ask this question, I'd probably have to spend the entire amount on earplugs so I might never hear it asked again.

The Jews of Europe were worried. They knew, as they read from the Sabbath Seder each week, "In each generation, they rise over us to destroy us." For reasons you've read about throughout this book, as I provide historical context for the development of Jewish Mysticism and its principal adherents, the Ashkenazi Hassidim, the Jews of Europe were accustomed to living in hostile environments.

However, despite the mounting aggression against Jews occasioned by Hitler's incessant rhetoric and despite the oppressions of Jews in violent response to it, nobody had any concept of the scale of the coming persecutions. Nobody could have known that a pogrom might become a national program of the attempted elimination of an identifiable religious group and others deemed "undesirable." The minds of these 20th Century Jewish people could not conceive of an entire continent being engulfed in the flames of a hatred so intense that it would devise new methods of removing Jews – not just from their shtetls – but from the face of the earth.

But it wasn't just the Jews who could not see the Holocaust coming. Despite Hitler's mounting campaigns of rhetorical and physical violence, containment, ghettoization, and socioeconomic prohibitions, there was little alarm expressed internationally.

In the enlightened and tolerant 20th Century (which came to be distinguished as the "Century of Genocide," for the Holocaust was one of many such attempted "ethnic cleansings"), genocide on this scale could not happen. People had become civilized of their more bestial impulses. That was generally believed about Hitler and his anti-Semitic campaign against the Jews – that is, it was rhetorical and oppressive but no more.

And that is why most did not run. Having seen the writing on the wall, only a few did as once the Prophet Saul had.

And so, for a moment, put yourselves in their shoes and ask yourselves why their neighbors and friends, often well-educated people, would so disguise themselves and accept the friendship and confidences of those they would watch eliminated. That is the unthinkable truth.

Where was God?

"God is at home. It's we who have gone out for a walk."

Meister Eckhart, (1260-1328), Theologian and Christian Mystic

Imagine surviving an event like the Holocaust.

Maybe you've woken up in the dark, crushed under the weight of numerous human bodies. You realize these are the dead and that to survive, you must crawl out from beneath them, terrified that the Nazis will return.

Or maybe you've been herded from the work camp and taken on a Death March in 20-degree winter weather as Allied liberators advanced. There is no food.

Or maybe you've witnessed the Nazis suddenly abandoning Majdanek, stunned knowing that your nightmare of state abuse is over.

It's not possible for any of us who weren't imprisoned in the camps to truly understand the depths of the horrors visited upon human life in them. We can scratch the surface, and we can probably ask ourselves where God might have been while all this monstrous evil was being loosed on the earth.

Had God abandoned the Israelites, grown tired and enraged at their failure to bring about the healing of the relationship? This caused many Jews to lose their faith in the wake of the Holocaust. The destruction of entire worlds, communities, and even the potential of tiny babies was a monumental, communal psychic and spiritual burden - one which continues to be borne by subsequent generations.

The Piercing Shards

With the lives of six million Jews consumed by the Holocaust, European Jewry lay in tattered ruins. Many repudiated any faith in God. For the Hassidim, this was a dual repudiation.

Because, in tandem with God, the Hassidim felt betrayed by the Tzadekkim. Considering what we read earlier about the Tzadek taking on the guilt of his followers, it's almost unbelievable that leaders in that tradition would flee, abandoning those they'd once lived as one with, in leadership.

And even before the Rebbes fled, they'd not been able to detect the coming of yet another assault on God's Chosen. Their roles as sages and leaders had effectively collapsed in the face of impending annihilation.

The Hassidic Tzadekkim counseled their followers to remain in place, advising against emigration to the United States, which they deemed, at the time, to be a treyfe (unclean) country. They further counseled against Aliyah (emigration to the Holy Land) in the face of Teodor Herzel's calls for Jews to return (Zionism, which was opposed in the community). And finally, the Rebbes told their followers not to adopt assimilation or its appearance to avoid detection.

The Tzadekkim told their followers to stay near them, and that's what happened. But then, these supposed leaders fled to save themselves, leaving behind their doomed communities. These included the Satmar, Gerer, Lubavitch, and Belzer Hassidim.

Hassidism's most vital center, Poland, had been almost completely eradicated, with only 15% of Polish Jews surviving the war. Even fewer of the Hassidim survived. Post-war Hassidism was broken beyond what many believed was the hope of renewal or repair.

Those who arrived in the USA came shattered and impoverished, having been stripped of any communal wealth by the voracious Nazis. They had no means to develop the educational resources they'd built up to such stature in the Old World or to maintain a truly Hassidic lifestyle, separated from the influence of the world around them while living in its midst.

And yet, like a miracle, Hassidism again rose from the ashes.

Post-War Diaspora

After the war, the world answered the horror of the Holocaust with the State of Israel, and many Jewish survivors made Aliyah, including the Hassidim. Some Hassidim went to Antwerp, Belgium, Montreal, Canada, or London, England, and established communities. But many Jews headed for the Statue of Liberty's home, with its invitation to the "poor, huddled masses" of the world.

And today, it's in New York City that we find the largest Jewish community in the world – outside of Israel. New York City is also home to the largest Hassidic Jewish community in the world, with representation from some of the most well-known and influential dynasties.

Of the 250,000 Hassidim estimated to be living in the world, 100,000 are in New York City, with the rest dispersed across the globe, some even in Russia and Eastern Europe.

The Lubavitcher Rebbe arrived in New York City in 1940, which perhaps explains the tremendous number of Lubavitcher Hassidim there. The influence of the Chabad organization, both in the USA and globally, is tremendous. Its presence in Israel is high profile, with the image of the Rebbe seen almost everywhere you go.

The Hassidim have a strong belief in the power of reproduction to restore what has been broken (whether by the power of Ohr Ein Sof or by the evil of man). The Hassidic family unit is, therefore, large. A Hassidic couple will usually have as many as eight children. This is a factor that doubled the Hassidic population of New York City in only 20 years.

But it's not just the reproductive fervor of the Hassidim that have swelled their numbers. Non-Hassidic Jews are turning to Hassidism as a more authentic way of living a life rooted in the Faith. Lubavitchers have a strong bent toward evangelizing to other, less orthodox (which means "right thinking") Jews, a unique feature of their communal beliefs.

The Hassidim in New York City

The Hassidim have only recently expanded into suburban areas, replicating the village life of Eastern Europe known by the pioneers of the modern movement. Because in NYC, the post-war drive to replace those lives lost to the Jewish World in the Holocaust has driven a tremendous population explosion among the Hassidim.

In 2012, the New York Times reported that the city's Jewish community had increased to 1.1 million, with much of that increase attributed to the urban Hassidic and other Haredi (which we'll be discussing shortly) communities. But in the 1950s, the population of NYC Jews was two million, and so a decline has been addressed by the Hassidim in a rather spectacular fashion.

About 40% of the Jews in New York City in the 2012 survey detailed in the article described themselves as Orthodox. This represents an increase of about 1/3, compared to the year 2002. Almost 75% of Jewish youth in NYC are from Orthodox families.

The story of the reanimation from the mountain of ashes left by the Holocaust's evils almost seems miraculous. But what it's about community cohesion, perseverance, and the drive to maintain beliefs passed on from generation to generation, Hassidic dynasty to Hassidic dynasty.

Once the kids in the black leather jackets, rebelling against the existing order, Hassidism has been transformed in its latest incarnation; resurrected with all its wounds in the physical trappings of earlier times. Rigidly dogmatic, politically activist, and determined in its ambitions, Ashkenazi Hassidim has come full circle in our times.

Haredi

Once enemies, the Hassidim and Mitnagdim, both opposed to the Jewish Enlightenment, allied in response. This alliance becomes the ultra-Orthodox movement of Judaism, most potently realized in New York City and the Holy Land.

Cleaving intimately to the tradition of Torah, the Haredi life is marked by the maintenance of the 613 mitzvot (commandments) and the scrupulous observance of halakhah (Jewish Law). Made visible through their unusual dress, they're known for several distinguishing characteristics:

- The men wear large, black hats (varying between communities), with their hair arranged in two coils of hair, one on each side of the head (payot). The kippa (yarmulka) is worn under the large hat.

- Adult males wear black suits, with a tallit (prayer shawl) visible and long, black, sometimes satin, coats (rekel).

- Adult males cultivate beards as soon as physically possible.

- Adult females are austerely dressed, in long skirts or dresses, but sometimes fashionably so. Pants are forbidden to be worn by women.

- Adult females shave their heads after marriage and wear wigs. The rationale is this underlines the woman's commitment to fidelity.

- Some adult females wear a snood or a scarf over their wigs

Traditional gendered roles are assigned according to sex, with the male in the position of family leader and the female the bearer and rearer of children, preparer of food, and general cook and bottle washer. The man is expected to further the healing of Creation via the mitzvot, teach and learn, and advance the community's interests, sometimes, politically.

The distinctive, religiously oriented dress of Haredi men is modeled after that of the Polish nobility in the 18th Century and is not mandated by scripture, related more to the historical setting than religious codes. Even the long black coat associated with Ultra-Orthodox men is derived from a Rabbinical decree in the 18th Century. This decree was issued, banning outerwear in any colors, as such finery might incite the jealousy of the gentiles.

Whether religiously derived or not, strict adherence to Haredi dress codes is enforced via communal policing of deviations and sometimes under the rabbinical discipline of various kinds. This strictness relates directly to the community's integrity, which is set apart from non-Jewish and non-Orthodox society.

The Haredi and Work

Because the Haredi culture is devoted to the study of sacred texts, the men have, traditionally, not worked. While this is rapidly changing, the unemployment rate among the Haredi community in Israel and the USA has become a social burden, necessitating the need for income to be generated. Haredi women have met this need.

In consideration of the gender roles associated with the community, this seems a reversal of internal regulation, but it has changed the fortunes of the community.

But the Haredi are also uniquely disadvantaged in the labor market, by their hand, due to the withdrawal from secular education. Educated only in the intricacies of Jewish religious literature after the age of 12, job opportunities tend to be limited, mostly, to religious leadership roles within the community.

Spending up to 12 hours every day in intense study and debate of sacred texts and Jewish Law, the ideal of the ultra-Orthodox Haredi is to live in a state of religious separatism and Holiness through the maintenance of halakhah, sustaining the family without feeling compelled to participate in the economy.

Numbering approximately one million, the Haredi of Israel largely live on a combination of state support and the community women's labor. Haredi women are now participating in the Israeli economy at the same rate as secular Jewish women. But because of the nature of the community, they work in lower-earning jobs, lacking the basic educational requirements to pursue higher paid work.

In Israel, due to the intervention of Prime Minister Ben-Gurion in 1940, the Haredi are not compelled to present themselves for military service. Created to exempt a handful of religious scholars, the legislation now covers over 30,000 members of the community. This is a profound departure from the international Jewish community's commitment to military service in Israel.

With an average birth rate of seven offspring per family, the Haredi are a growing presence in Israel. This is building tensions rooted in generalized resentment of the status of the ultra-Orthodox in secular Israeli society. With the Haredi population growing, Israelis are questioning the influence exerted by the group on societal issues. This minority, despite its contraction from the rest of Israeli society, has regularly been vocal in advancing its beliefs about legislation concerning national regulations governing the Sabbath and even the institution of marriage.

The Haredi are answering that resentment by reaching for alternatives. For example, many work in National Security, as their intense religious study prepares them for the tedious work of fine-combing Israeli intelligence documents. Some Haredi has also become tech entrepreneurs in this thriving sector of the Israeli economy. As we've read in this book, NLP was first employed in the project of apprehending the meaning of numbers in relationship to language (gematria) in the religious texts, so that seems quite logical.

There is also even a unique unit in the Israeli military for Haredim who choose to serve, which accommodates the needs of the community about study and kosher food. Within the community, there is a change. The Haredim are discovering that the 21st Century has demands that the 18th Century couldn't possibly have foreseen. While change is slow, it's emerging as the Haredim gradually integrate into Israeli society.

The NYC Haredi

Because we're talking about the same community with the same rules, here I'd like to offer a contemporary example of how Haredi's beliefs have run up against the needs of the society they live in, especially in NYC concerning COVID-19.

Why won't the Haredi cooperate with public health protocols, causing the virus to rage through the community at an uncontrollable rate?

It's important to understand, in this discussion, that the Haredi don't avail themselves of modern telecommunication in most cases. There is no television and no internet permitted usually. Most Haredi, while using cell phones, do so on a restricted basis, which precludes the use of functions deemed potentially dangerous.

Being a separatist religious expression, the prohibition against media consumption essentially deprived the Haredi of information about the virus when it spread across the globe in February and March.

And when the government intervened in the Haredim's refusal to comply with pandemic mandates, police became involved. This occurred both in Jerusalem and New York City. But it's the NYC example that has received the lion's share of media attention.

On April 28, 2020, a prominent Rabbi's funeral drew hundreds into the streets of Williamsburg, a borough of New York City heavily populated by the Haredi. The Rabbi's death was connected to the virus, but because of the secrecy of the Haredi, it's hard to know exactly how.

The funeral and the crowd that attended was broken up with the Mayor of NYC, Bill de Blasio, openly dressing down the community. Already resented, the response of the Haredi to the COVID-19 virus has raised the level of the secular world's hostility in the confrontation of Haredi separatism. It has highlighted the impracticality of setting oneself apart in a predominantly secular metropolis.

While the Haredi are neither anti-science nor anti-intellectual, they are highly motivated to seek allies, and with the rise of Donald Trump, they have seen such an ally in their refusal to conform to norms imposed by the government – even if it means lives lost in the community. The outgoing President's steadfast insistence on not requiring masks or social distancing as the virus raged was justification for the Haredi refusal to comply.

And this refusal has garnered critical attention as the infection rate in the United States again rises to alarming levels. For the Haredi, this attention represents media bias working in concert with secular society's biases against their beliefs and lifestyle. In it, they see the destruction of the Temples, the Crusades, the pogroms, and of course, the Holocaust. And the refusal of the Haredi to comply has spread beyond the ultra-Orthodox community in New York City to non-Orthodox communities beyond the city.

But the non-compliance of the Haredi community in the confrontation of COVID-19 is more complex than mere anti-Semitism. It doesn't matter if a community lives walled off from the greater society or not. A refusal to acknowledge a public health emergency, whether misinformed due to the prohibition of telecommunications in Haredi homes or willfully refusing to see the danger of a virus that can kill, brings calamity to that community but from arising from its own beliefs and practices.

Just as the Hassidic Rabbis of pre-war Europe advised their congregations to stay near them as the march of German Fascism threatened their very existence, Haredi leaders must confront their role in exposing their communities to this virus under the guise of defending Jewish Law.

Where is the Haredi Tzadek who will find the kernel of guilt within himself to deliver his community and others from the shadow of the pandemic? That Tzadek would be honoring the traditions on which Haredi culture is built by prioritizing and thus protecting the community for which he is responsible.

Modernity Knocks

In the 21st Century, the ultra-Orthodox and the Hassidim who now fall under their umbrella, find themselves at a crossroads. As their communities burgeon, they butt up against the walls they've built around themselves.

Those walls, constructed in the service of preventing the pollution of the community by the world's evil, could not prevent COVID-19 from slipping in under cover of the worldly darkness most feared by the Haredi.

In Israel, the Haredi are less than 10% of the total population, and yet they account for over 40% of all infections.

Defying lockdowns during the Jewish Holidays, the Haredi have gathered in large groups and have packed synagogues, while ultra-Orthodox schools have remained open.

In NYC, Governor Cuomo responded to outbreaks centered in Haredi neighborhoods like Borough Park by closing synagogues and non-essential businesses. As a result, protests by the ultra-Orthodox rocked Borough Park for three consecutive nights in October 2020. As part of the protests, masks were set on fire, involving about 100 of the Haredi protesters, who were originally there to attend a rally for Donald Trump. A man videotaping the demonstration was beaten unconscious by the angry mob.

While history informs us as to the reluctance of the Haredi to conform to worldly authority, there is the communities' resolute naivete implicated to accept that government has its best interests at heart. There is also a reluctance to connect the health of their communities to that of the non-Orthodox and non-Jewish communities with which they share the city.

Far from the 18th Century shtetls of Eastern Europe, New York is a high-density city. Being set apart, while a religiously mandated part of being Haredi, is a mean feat in such a setting, and that is modernity's knock at the gate of ultra-Orthodoxy.

This has become abundantly clear in the recent increase in COVID-19 in ultra-Orthodox areas of NYC, namely Brooklyn and Queens. While making up only 7% of the city's population, over 25% of all new infections are among the Haredim. And while the infection rate in New York state is at about 1%, in these community hot spots, the rate of infection is 5%.

For the Hassidim, the word and instruction of the Tzedek is everything. From interpreting the world through the lens of halakhah, it's the leaders of the communities gathered under the Haredi umbrella who set the tone and pace of community responses to crises like these.

But with the Tzadekkim ignoring the need to protect their communities, just as they did before the Second World War, this version of modernity and the peril it's brought with it may again destroy the Temple. When the Temple lives in the people, where else may it be built?

Conclusion

I hope you've found the information you're seeking in this book. While small in scope, I've attempted to include as much context and information as possible toward introducing Jewish Mysticism, its texts, and the community most responsible for disseminating them.

It's also my hope that you won't stop seeking, as the world of Jewish Mysticism is vast. Imagine that the Haredi spent up to 12 hours every day studying the halakhah – a discipline they practice throughout their lives. There is nothing simple about this corner of Judaism. It is complex, but it's also incredibly rewarding and illuminating.

I thank you for reading. Now, I leave you with the words of the Baal Shem Tov, founder of Ashkenazi Hassidism.

"Your fellow man is your mirror. If your face is clean, the image you perceive will also be flawless. But should you look upon your fellow man and see a blemish, it is your imperfection that you are encountering - you are being shown what it is that you must correct within yourself."

Here's another book by Mari Silva that you might like

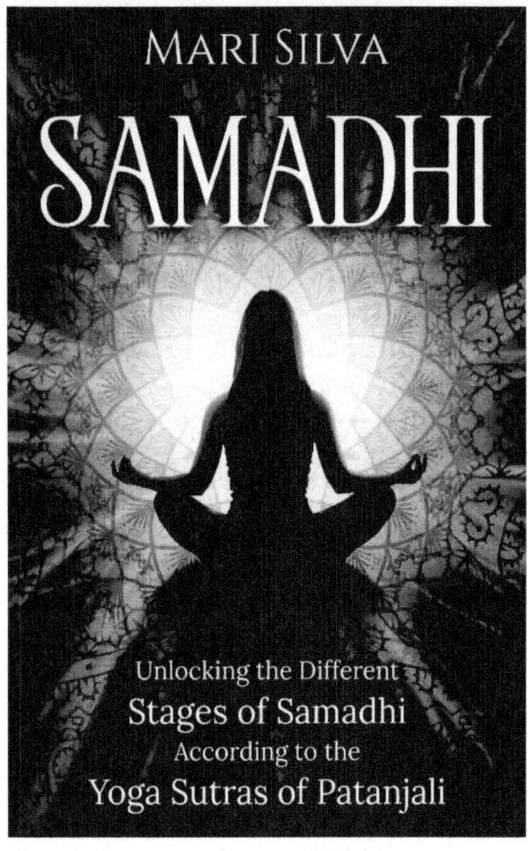

Your Free Gift (only available for a limited time)

Thanks for getting this book! If you want to learn more about various spirituality topics, then join Mari Silva's community and get a free guided meditation MP3 for awakening your third eye. This guided meditation mp3 is designed to open and strengthen ones third eye so you can experience a higher state of consciousness. Simply visit the link below the image to get started.

https://spiritualityspot.com/meditation

References

Jewish Mysticism. (n.d.). People.Ucalgary.Ca.
https://people.ucalgary.ca/~elsegal/RelS369/B04c_MedievalMysticism.html

Judaism - Sefer yetzira. (n.d.). Encyclopedia Britannica. Retrieved from
https://www.britannica.com/topic/Judaism/Sefer-yetzira

ResearchGate | Share and discover research. (2019). ResearchGate; ResearchGate.
https://www.researchgate.net/

(N.d.). https://www.amazon.com/Trends-Jewish-Mysticism-Gershom-Scholem-
ebook/dp/B004JHYSCQ/ref=sr_1_5

Printed in Great Britain
by Amazon

62799637R00070